Contents

ISBN-0-87666-694-2

Distributed in the U.S. by T.F.H. Publications, Inc., 211 West
Sylvania Avenue, PO Box 427, Neptune, NJ 07753; in
England by T.F.H. (Gt. Britain) Ltd., 13 Nutley Lane, Reigate,
Surrey; in Canada to the book store and library trade by
Beaverbooks Ltd., 150 Lesmill Road, Don Mills, Ontario M38
2T5, Canada; in Canada to the pet trade by Rolf C. Hagen
Ltd., 3225 Sartelon Street, Montreal 382, Quebec; in
Southeast Asia by Y.W. Ong, 9 Lorong 36 Geylang,
Singapore 14; in Australia and the South Pacific by Pet Im-
ports Pty. Ltd., P.O. Box 149, Brookvale 2100, N.S.W.
Australia; in South Africa by Valid Agencies, P.O. Box 51901,
Randburg 2125 South Africa. Published by T.F.H. Publica-
tions, Inc., Ltd, the British Crown Colony of Hong Kong.

Ibizan Hounds

By Joan McDonald Brearley

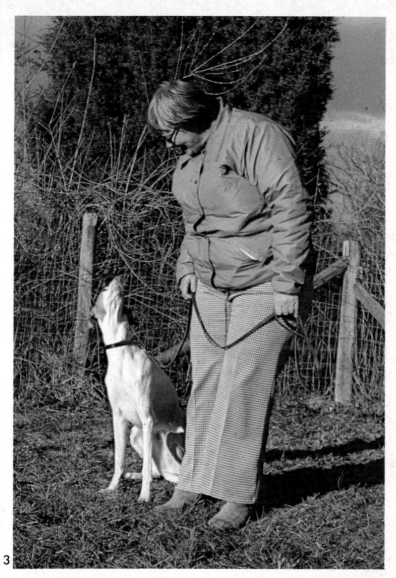

(1) An Ibizan at full run. The lean, muscular Ibizan Hound is a very swift dog, well suited to competition in coursing trials. (2) With an active dog such as the Ibizan, it is wise to keep yours out of doors as much as possible, in a fenced-in area such as this one, so the dog may run about at will. (3) A loving, trusting bond develops between the Ibizan and the person who spends the most time with it.

Photo credits: Our magnificent **cover** is Ishtar's Pico of Al-Yram, owned by Kurt Kroll of Hawthorne, NJ. Photo by Aaron Norman. **Back cover** photo, of Charlotte Schwartz' O'Bre-On's Gyrfalcon Brandy Lane, by Ron Reagan. Pp. 2-3, 6, 7, 10, 11, 14(2), 15, 114, 115, 118, 119, 122, 123, 126-127 by Ron Reagan. Following photos compiled by author: frontispiece, 12, 14(1), 16 through 47, 117, 121, 124. Mr. Reagan's photos courtesy of Charlotte Schwartz, Brandy Lane Farm Kennel, Mt. Holly, NJ. Ms. Schwartz' Ibizan appearing in the photos is O'Bre-On's Gyrfalcon Brandy Lane, T.D. **Frontispiece:** Ishtar Sonnet of Loki, C.D. and field champion. Sonnet won her obedience title in three consecutive trials and was undefeated in the breed in the Miscellaneous classes. She is owned by Susan Stafford, Crest Park, Cal.

Ibizan is pronounced Ah-*Beez*-an

Dedication

To the memory of

BOBBEE LEE PREU

who introduced me to the beauty of the

Ibizan Hounds

and to

RHODA LOW SEOANE

who with her late husband

Consuelo Andrew Seoane

brought the first Ibizan Hounds to the United States

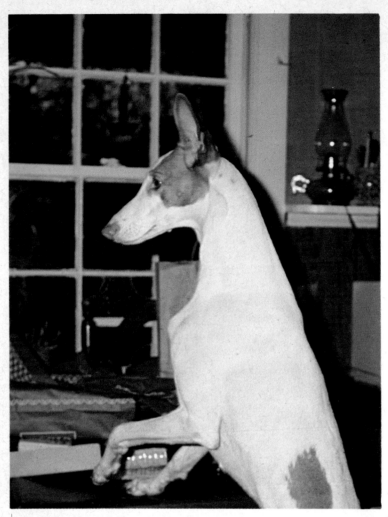

1

Shown are two photos which illustrate the alert curiosity of the breed. The Ibizan Hound is a highly intelligent breed, and one that will want to be a part of all the goings-on around the household! In (1), we see Charlotte Schwartz' young female, O'Bre-On's Gyrfalcon Brandy Lane, T.D. peering curiously out of a window. Gyrfalcon has the distinction of being the first and only Ibizan Hound tracking dog in the world. (2) Here, Gyrfalcon gazes up at something that has caught her fancy.

2 →

1. THE IBIZAN: HOUND OF ANTIQUITY

It was in 1956 that the first Ibizan Hounds reached American shores. After more than two decades of selective breeding and promotion by a group of dedicated fanciers, the Ibizan Hound became the 124th breed of dog to be registerable with the American Kennel Club. The goal was reached on January 1, 1979. While the Ibizan Hounds are one of the newest breeds eligible to compete in the championship classes at dog shows, they are believed to be one of the oldest breeds in existence today.

Admirers of the Ibizan have researched these smooth, sleek and sure-footed canine aristocrats and are agreed that the breed dates back to the pre-Christian era in the land of the Nile River. Pictures and carvings in caves and on walls of the tombs of the great pharaohs in Egypt bear remarkable likenesses to the Ibizan Hounds of today.

As far back as 3400 B.C., remains of dogs of similar conformation to the Ibizan were found in the tomb of Hemaka. Hemaka reigned during Egypt's first dynasty (3100-2700 B.C.) and in his tomb there are hunting scenes on the walls which portray dogs of this type seizing goats by their throats. Likenesses of Ibizans bringing down ibex are depicted in wall scenes in the tomb of Ptolomy, and in the tomb of Nefermat, dating back to the fourth dynasty (2650 B.C.) the dogs are catching foxes by their tails during a chase.

In 1922, when the tomb of the boy-king, Tutankhamon (reign: 1366-1357 B.C.) was unearthed in Egypt's Valley of the Kings, graven images of Anubis, Watchdog of the Dead, were found. The entrance to Tut's tomb was guarded by a life-size statue of Anubis, lending further evidence that it was an Ibizan that was worshipped as "the dog of the Pharaohs."

It is written that Cleopatra (reign: 51-30 B.C.) had several of these "Egyptian Greyhounds," the prick-eared, ring-tailed dogs that were call-

Opposite: A famous dog from the early days in this country . . . Col. and Mrs. Consuelo Seoane's Tripol de Jamma-Nura, bred in the kennels of the Marquesa Belgida in Spain.

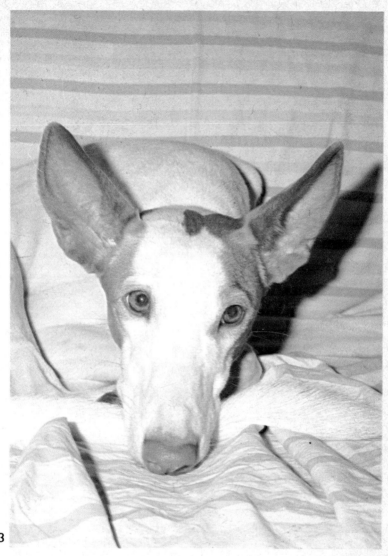

3

(1) Sylvan Willow of O'Bre-On's, shown as a pup, and owned by Kathleen O'Brien. This impressive specimen illustrates the alert curiosity of the breed. (2) An Ibizan Hound striking a noble pose while at rest in a field, gazing into the distance as if in memory of its ancient heritage, as sentry to the pharaohs of Egypt. Here, this Ibizan pauses from munching on a healthful nylon bone. (3) The characteristic facial expression showing one of the Ibizan's many moods is depicted here.

ed Galgos. Ancient Roman coins also featured a likeness of the dogs we know as Ibizan Hounds.

It is the island of Ibiza to which the Ibizan owes its present name. The Phoenicians, Romans, Carthaginians, Moors and other early traders who sailed the Mediterranean Sea in the eighth or ninth centuries carried the dogs from Egypt to Ibiza, the small Balearic island off the coast of Spain. Legend has it that the Ibizan Hound rode atop Hannibal's elephants as the Carthaginian general invaded Italy by crossing the Alps. The fact that Hannibal, who lived from 247-138 B.C. was born on Ibiza adds to the likelihood of this tale, and accounts for the Ibizan's being referred to at times as "Hannibal's dog."

The Ibizan Hound has had several other names down through the centuries, and even today it is known by other names. In Ibiza they are called the *Podenco Ibicenco,* "the dog with the air of a doe," and in other Balearic islands where the Catalan language is spoken they are called *Ca Eivissencs.*

ISLAND HUNTERS

On Ibiza these dogs have always been used as hunters for rabbits and other small game. The shortage of food on this tiny island at one time made it necessary for the inhabitants to have a dog of great stamina

A photograph of a portion of a wall in an unearthed Egyptian tomb featuring a hunting dog bearing a strong likeness to the Ibizan Hound. Said to be "the oldest dog in the world," the Ibizan Hound is a descendant of these Egyptian hunting dogs dating back thousands of years.

Guindola de Jamma-Nura, one of the early Ibizans in Spain. Photograph courtesy of Rhoda Low Seoane, from her personal collection.

and keen hunting instincts who would help in acquiring food. The Ibizan Hound is renowned for these very traits. With food at such a premium, not all the puppies in a given litter could be fed and the weaker ones—and mostly the males—were drowned in the sea. Those which were allowed to survive had to learn to fend for themselves if the meager diet of fish heads and an occasional bit of goat meat did not suffice. Most of the rabbits which the dogs hunted went to feed the people. The virtual isolation of Ibiza and the neighboring island of Formentera just nine miles away kept them breeding sound and true for more than 5,000 years.

THE IBIZAN IN SPAIN

As civilization marched on and tourism expanded to include even the smaller Mediterranean islands, it was inevitable that the elegant Ibizan Hounds would catch the eyes of visitors to Ibiza. Fortunately, they came to the attention of Dona Maria Dolores Olives de Cotonera, the Marquesa de Belgida of Barcelona. The breed could not have found a better or more dedicated advocate than the Marquesa, a dog show judge and a highly respected authority on dogs.

The Marquesa's rigid and well-planned breeding program kept the quality of the breed high once she introduced it in Spain. While her kennels were on another Balearic island, Majorca, it was in Spain that her

17

Pharaoh, owned by W.R. Reynolds and photographed in December of 1970. Whelped in Canada during May of 1965, his sire was Casita ex Perra de Ibiza. Photo courtesy of Ron and Judy Bauer.

champions were shown to their titles, and she saw to it that all of her stock was registered with the Royal Canine Society of Spain. One of her rough-coated Ibizan Hounds held championship titles in France and Portugal as well as in Spain.

The Marquesa de Belgida also supervised the selection of Ibizan Hounds which were to be sent to the United States in the early days of importation here, making sure that American bloodlines started off with the best available stock. In 1978 she was asked to draw up a new standard for the breed by the Royal Canine Society of Madrid, and is still recognized as the leading authority on the breed.

Shortly after the Ibizan Hound's popularity was established in Spain, the breed found its way to other countries in Europe. It was seen at dog shows, on race tracks and hunting or coursing in the fields. Interest in the Ibizan became so widespread that in 1958 the Egyptian government sent a special commission to Ibiza and to the island of Formentera to check on the breed. While there, the members of the commission purchased top specimens of the breed to bring back to Egypt, reintroducing the Ibizan Hound in its native land.

One of the "early greats" of the breed: Phaedra, owned by Mrs. William C. Thompson.

2. THE IBIZAN HOUND IN AMERICA

During the mid 1950's, when United States Signal Corps Colonel and Mrs. Consuelo Andrew Seoane returned from Ibiza and settled in Bristol, Rhode Island, the first Ibizan Hounds reached American shores. The Seoanes' "Hannibal" and "Cetera," bred by Vincente Cardon of San Rafael, Ibiza, arrived in April, 1956. A litter of "Stop's" and "Tanit's," the first litter to be bred in America, was whelped in September of that same year.

There were four males and four females in that litter and their names were "Asunicon," "Malchus V," "Denia," "Heulalia," "Granada," "Mago," "Gisco" and "Sertorius." One of these puppies went to the Spanish Ambassador in Washington, D.C. Granada went to Helen Peck, prominent as an officer in the national breed club and in helping to gain recognition for the breed in those early days. Helen Peck maintains her interest today.

From the original two imports, Hannibal and Certera, several later imports from Ibiza came to the Seoane's Ivicene Kennels. In addition to six specimens imported from Ibiza via Barcelona in January, 1957, named "Curra," "Dama," "Florita," "Falco," "Paloma," and "Corredor," others were to follow shortly to further enhance the Seoanes' breeding program. "Sil" and "Garbo" were purchased the following year from Señor Don Pedro Olives Carreras, who had been breeding Ibizans since 1908.

All were registered with the Real Sociedad Canina, or Royal Canine Society, as important an organization there as the American Kennel Club is in this country. It was from these imports that our American Ibizan Hound stock has evolved.

In 1957, with the guidance and enthusiasm of the Seoanes and several other Ibizan Hound admirers, the Ibizan Hound Club of America was formed. Consuelo Seoane served as its first president. He was to continue

Opposite: The magnificent Malchus V, first male Ibizan Hound born in the U.S., in autumn of 1956. Malchus was bred by Mr. and Mrs. Consuelo Seoane from the first pair of Ibizans imported to this country, and was owned by Mr. and Mrs. Fred Lee Preu of Islesboro, Maine.

The first two Ibizan Hounds in America! Hannibal and Cetera, imported in 1956 by Consuelo Andrew Seoane and his artist wife, Rhoda Low Seoane. These two dogs served as the foundation stock for the Seoanes' Ivicene Kennels in Bristol, Rhode Island, and were behind the early Ibizan Hound breeding in this country.

in this office until his death in 1964, at which time his artist wife, Rhoda Low Seoane, took over for him. The Marquesa de Belgida was made an honorary vice president of the club. Ron Bauer served as the editor of "On the Run," the club's excellent newsletter.

The late Mr. and Mrs. Frederick Lee Preu of Washington, D.C. and Islesboro, Maine, were two other dedicated fanciers in the early days of the breed here. They purchased "Malchus V," the only male survivor in the Seoane's first litter, to be the foundation stud at their kennel. Over the succeeding years Fred and his wife Bobbee did much to help popularize the breed in this country.

Bobbee spared no effort or expense in making sure the Ibizans were seen all over the nation's capitol in the company of senators, ambassadors, and other important government people, as she waged a remarkable public relations campaign for the breed, from the couple's residence in Georgetown, Maryland. She supported the breed in the miscellaneous classes at dog shows in keen competition along the East Coast.

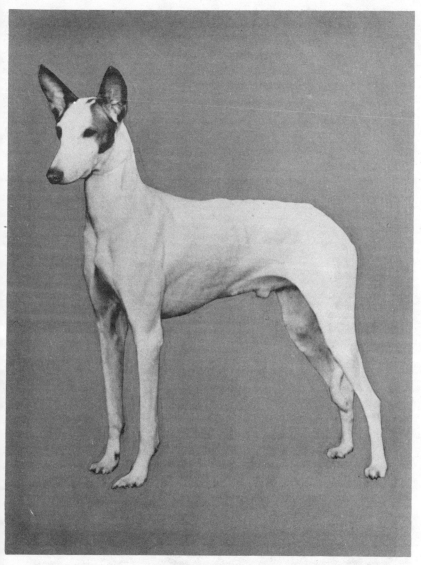

The top-winning Ibizan Hound in America for 1974 and 1975 was Eridu Maestro, owned and shown by Richard and Laura Edwards, Ishtar Ibizans, Phoenix, Arizona. "Maya," an English import, is a Champion in Mexico, and was featured in a recent issue of *Dog World* Magazine as the Ibizan which best represented the "ideal" for the breed. In 1977 eight out of ten of the "top ten" Ibizans in this country were his sons and daughters.

Granada, bitch from the first litter whelped in the United States. Sired by Hannibal out of Tanit, she was owned by Helen Peck of Rhode Island in the 1950's.

While editor of *Popular Dogs* magazine, I invited Bobbee Preu to write several articles during the 1960's and 70's on this fascinating breed.

Bobbee's "Preu Sampson" became one of the first obedience titled dogs in this country. The Preus were to breed several generations of fine Ibizan Hounds. The names of their kennels and their dogs can be found behind many of today's top contenders in the show ring as well as the field. The breed suffered a great loss with the untimely passing, in the 1970's, of these two stalwart advocates.

HUNTING IN IBIZA

In 1959 an American writer, Stetson Kennedy, went to the island of Ibiza and first caught sight of the local *Podenco Ibicencos*. He met Señor

Opposite: Field champion Gallantree's Road Runner, pictured at 16 months of age in his racing colors. Here, Road Runner and his owner-trainer, Nan Kilgore Koppel, wait patiently for the next race.

Preux Sampson, pictured finishing for his Companion Dog title in May 1970. Owners Ron and Judy Bauer, Gallantree Kennels, Florissant, Colorado. A Ritter photograph.

Jaime Mari Escandell, from the neighboring island of Formentera, who was considered an authority on the breed. Stetson was eager to learn all he could about the unusual breed, and when Señor Escandell invited him on a hunt with four of his dogs, he quickly accepted.

Stetson learned that no guns are necessary for hunting on Ibiza. The Ibizans can be counted on to always return the catch to their masters. The Ibizans that are hunted with by sportsmen are trained to merely retrieve, without actually making a kill. Ibizans make excellent retrievers and are equally successful on day or night forays. They hunt by sight, sound and scent.

26

The top coursing Ibizan for 1976 was Treybeau Spanish Flyer. Flyer, who was the #1 Lure Courser for two years, is owned by Nan Kilgore Koppel of Baltimore, Maryland.

The perfect profile: Cass, an Ibizan Hound from the Ishtar Kennels of Richard and Laura Edwards of Phoenix, Arizona.

The pattern of hunting used by the Ibizan Hounds who are to supply their masters with food is for them to find the prey in the brush, circle it, bark until they have flushed it, chase it, catch it, kill it with one snap of the neck, bring it to the master, and be off again for the next!

The Ibizan Hounds' short coats, thin bodies and extreme agility make it easy for them to track their prey up and over fences, or down and under all kinds of brush. They excel at both high and broad jumping and, should they lose sight of their prey, they are known to stand on their hind legs until it is sighted again. Their hind leg stances are well known to their owners. Also, Ibizans are able to jump six to eight feet straight up in the air from a standstill position! Their facility to maneuver and be at ease in an upright position is likened to the Alexandrian dog-god, Hermanubis, pictured on the walls of the Egyptian tombs in an upright position, and resembles the Ibizan in every way.

Collosi Seti, while not shown, was Jane Wilcoxson's first Ibizan Hound, and the one that endeared the breed to her. Jane has been active in and devoted to the breed for many years.

The late Bobbee Preu with two four-month-old Ibizans, Jeremiah, the male, and Zorina, the female. Their illustrious grandsire was Malchus V, bred by the Seoanes and the foundation stud at the Preus' Ibizans of Islesboro Kennels in Maine.

Although the Ibizans hunt primarily rabbits and small game in the areas around the Mediterranean sea, their hunting instinct enables them to bring down animals as large as deer and bobcats. Once again, recall the hunting scenes in the Egyptian tombs where the dogs are shown in pursuit of gazelle, ibex, foxes and other animals indigenous to the lands along the Nile. Indeed, Ibizans are such eager hunters that in these Mediterranean countries they are sometimes shackled with a chain securing a front leg to a back leg so that they cannot take off to hunt on their own.

When Stetson Kennedy returned to America, he was surprised and delighted to read an advertisement in a New York City newspaper offering a pair of Ibizans for sale. The ad led to John West, who had brought "Luna," an all-white female, and "Arraco," a red and white male back to the United States with him from Ibiza. It was necessary at that time for John to return to Ibiza, and the dogs had to be sold. Stetson purchased both dogs and drove his first two Ibizan Hounds to his Florida home, where they were to hunt and thrive in the wilds of his 50 acre estate for years to come. Several other Ibizans of Stetson's breeding were to come along in the years that followed.

Stetson has served as secretary of the Ibizan Hound Club of America; a member of the world Federation of Ibizan Hound Fanciers; and he authored several articles promoting the breed. Several of these articles were published in *Popular Dogs* magazine.

29

3. IBIZAN CHARACTERISTICS AND STANDARD

Aside from their hunting instincts, now known to be almost beyond comparison, Ibizan Hounds also make excellent guard and watch dogs. Their enormous, erect ears make for keen hearing, and while they do not bark unnecessarily, they are quick to sound a warning at the approach of strangers.

Their great speed and agility is another of the breed's outstanding characteristics. When raced in Europe over the years, they have been clocked at speeds up to 40 miles an hour. This clearly puts them in a class with the racing Greyhounds, Salukis, Afghan Hounds and Borzoi, all of which have been known to reach equally impressive speeds in the field and on the track. There has been talk of racing them even more extensively in this country now that they have proven their ability in the open fields.

While it can be said that the Ibizans are an active, adventurous breed, they are in no way nervous or skittish dogs. The young are sturdy and curious, and all Ibizans remain playful throughout their adult years. And, ever frisky, they have a charming way of clicking their teeth at each other to encourage play.

Ibizan conformation presents yet another comparison to the Greyhound. Said to be the prototype of the earliest Egyptian Greyhounds, Ibizans are obviously of slightly heavier bone. In motion, their movement has been compared to the graceful Afghan Hounds and the Salukis. But even after all the past centuries of being likened to and compared with various other breeds they are unquestionably a breed unto themselves, with their more outstanding feature being their magnificent heads. Few can resist the breed's intelligent expression, with large ears pointing straight forward and small, oblique, amber eyes. Their long,

Opposite: Sunking Eterna of Treybeau, the first Ibizan to become a field champion in the United States. Just 14 months of age when she gained her field title, Eterna was a tender 11 months of age when she became a champion of the Ibizan Hound Club of the United States. She is co-owned by Dean Wright and Kathy O'Brien. Photograph by Sharon Gaudet.

Bobbee Preu with eight-month-old Jeremiah and 14-month-old Preux Sampson at her Ibizans of Isleboro Kennels in Maine. Photographed in November of 1968, these were two of the stud dogs at this pioneer kennel established in the 1950's. Even though seen here at a young age, Jeremiah and Sampson exemplify the excellence that is called for in the breed standard. They are both outstanding specimens and as such have earned great fame in the breed.

Jane Wilcoxson's striking Ibizan Hound, Gallantree's Princess Senuwy. Photograph by Ted Koppel.

strong muzzles and pink or flesh-colored noses add to their striking appearance. No other breed has this unusual color combination. Their exceptionally long, arched necks, a straight topline and sickle-shaped tails with white tips add to the overall appearance of strength and power.

While the smooth, short-coated Ibizan Hounds are by far the most popular and common variety of Ibizan all over the world, there are three different types of coat textures in the breed. In addition to the smooth, there are wirehaired and the long, or rough-coated varieties. Occasionally, these variations crop up in a litter, and in Europe they are bred back to the short-coated dogs and are also exhibited in the show ring without penalty. Coat texture is purely a matter of personal preference among breeders.

The Ibizan can be solid red, or solid lion-color, but either of these two colors mixed with white in a sort of "pinto pattern" are the most common. Usually, the color is divided on the head, and features a colored diamond-shaped spot between the ears and above the eyes. This is sometimes referred to as an "ax mark" or "third eye." Eye color is similar to coat color, lion-colored dogs having the true amber shade while the reds might tend to carry a slightly darker, or caramel tone.

The Ibizan's height at the shoulders ranges from 23½ inches to 27½ inches, with the females being slightly smaller than the males. Their weight varies from 42 to 50 pounds, again depending on sex.

STANDARD FOR THE IBIZAN HOUND

Head: Long and narrow, in the form of a sharp cone truncated at its base; extremely dry-fleshed. **Skull:** Long and flat, prominent occipital bone, little defined stop; narrow brow. **Ears:** Prominent prick ears, always rigid; erect on alert, but highly mobile and at times pointed forward, sideways, or backward, according to mood. The center of the base is at the level of the eyes, and in the form of an enlarged rhomboid truncated at a third of its longer diagonal. Thin, with texture of fine leather; no hair in interior. **Eyes:** Oblique and small, ranging in color from clear amber to caramel; aspect intelligent and unpredictable. **Muzzle:** Elongated, fine, and slender, sometimes snipy; very light Roman convex. Length from eyes to point of nose equal to distance from eyes to occiput. **Nose:** Prominent, extending beyond lower jaw; flesh color tending to harmonize with that of coat; nostrils open. **Jaws:** Exceptionally strong, lean. **Lips:** Thin and tight. **Teeth:** Level mouth; teeth perfectly opposed in scissor-bite; white and well-set.

Neck: Long, slender, slightly arched; strong, yet flat-muscled. **Withers:** Loose and detached. **Shoulders:** Sloping.

Back: Level and straight; taut yet elastic. **Loins:** Medium breadth, slightly arched. **Rump:** Very slightly sloping. **Tail:** Long, set rather low; highly mobile, and carried in sickle, ring, otter or saber positions according to mood and individual specimen.

Chest: Deep and long; breastbone sharply angled and very prominent; flat ribs, protruding when dog is in top working condition. **Belly:** Underbelly retracted, but not so deeply as Greyhound.

Forequarters: Straight front; forearms very long, strong, straight and close, lying flat on chest and continuing in straight line to ground. Clean fine bone; well-developed sinews; pasterns straight and flexible.

Hindquarters: Relatively vertical; strong but flat-muscled; hocks strong and close to ground.

Feet: Hare-foot; toes long and closed, very strong; interdigital spaces well protected by hair; durable pads.

Coat: **Short;** shortest on head and ears and longest at back of thighs and under tail. **Wire-Haired;** can be from one to three inches in length with a possible generous moustache, more hair on back, back of thighs and tail. Both types of coat are always hard in texture. Neither coat is preferable to the other.

Color: Red and white, red with white, white with red, lion and white, lion with white, white with lion; solid white, solid red; all other colors excluded. The preponderant pattern is predominantly red, with white feet and "socks", tail tip, chest, and muzzle, with blaze on forehead. The solid colors are desirable but relatively rare.

Height: Height of dogs at withers ranges from 23½ to 27½ inches; height of bitches at withers ranges from 22½ to 26 inches. Sizes somewhat over or under norms not to be regarded as demerits when other qualities are good. **Weight:** Average weight of dogs, 50 pounds; bitches, 42 to 49 pounds.

Preux Delilah's Jezabel, owned by Susan Stafford and bred by the late Bobbee Preu. Sired by Preux Jeremiah de Faholo ex Preux Electra de Faholo, Jezabel was one of the early Ibizan Hound greats in this country.

Left: Preux Ptolemy, a big winner during the 1960's in the Miscellaneous Classes. Breeder-owner-handler Bobbee Preu was a familiar figure in the show ring with this unusual breed new to the U.S., and she did much to establish the breed here. Below: Kreskin Kharisma of O'Bre-On, C.D. owned by Kathy O'Brien. Kreskin was undefeated in the breed during his ring career.

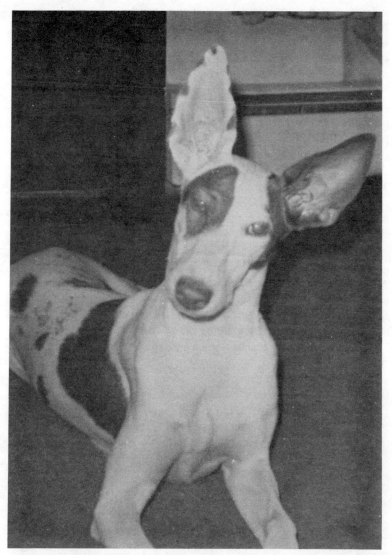

Black Chip's Gypsy of Loki, field champion owned by Mary Ann Blair of Ocean City, New Jersey. Note the curious, intelligent expression of Gypsy, and the alert prick ears, one of the breed's hallmarks. Gypsy bears the distinct look that has garnered Ibizans much attention wherever they go, whether gaiting in show rings, coursing on a track, or simply walking on lead with their masters.

Gait: A trot in suspension; elegant and graceful in the manner of the Afghan. In speed the Ibizan is in the same class as other coursing breeds, and is without equal in agility and high-jumping ability, being capable of springing to great heights from a standstill.

Down through the centuries, Ibizans have managed to maintain their even tempers and marvelous dispositions. Their desire for human companionship has in no way meant sacrificing any of their natural ability to perform efficiently in the field. They are adaptable to both warm and cold climates, though after so many years in the warm Mediterranean climate, where it seldom rains, they are not overly fond of wet weather. They are extremely clean dogs, and spend a great deal of time cleaning themselves in much the same manner as cats do. Therefore, extreme care must be taken to protect them from chemically treated collars and pesticides.

Grooming an Ibizan Hound requires little extra care to keep them looking sleek. A good brushing with a natural bristle brush a couple of times a week; trimming the nails; cleaning the ears; and occasionally cleaning the teeth is all that is necessary. For show dogs, a bath, preferably with a shampoo made especially for white dogs (if the dog is mostly white); towel or blow drying; and trimming the whiskers the day of the show is all the additional care that is needed before the dog's appearance in a show ring.

Ibizan Hounds are known to be good whelpers, with litters averaging from seven to 10 puppies. However, there have been exceptional litters. Kathy O'Brien of California reports that her bitch, "Aquilla," whelped a litter of 20 in May, 1977, eight females and 12 males. Her kennel population rose from two to 22 in 10½ hours. As far as is known, this is the world record for the breed. A photograph of the dam and her brood appeared in an issue of *The Gazehound.*

4. THE NEW IBIZAN PUPPY

PREPARING FOR THE PUPPY'S ARRIVAL

In choosing a puppy, be certain beforehand that each member of the family is truly enthusiastic about having this particular breed of dog as an addition to their circle. Dogs are much too intelligent not to sense whether or not they are liked. If your puppy feels unwanted, you may find an unhappy dog on your hands that could easily turn into a "problem child." Before buying, research the breed and make sure it is the one for you. Besides reading, a good way to learn about your prospective pet is to observe one of the same breed in its permanent home surroundings. Most owners will be only too happy to show off their furry friend.

One of the most important factors to consider when selecting a dog, whether it is to be a pet or show dog, is its temperament. When looking at a litter of puppies for a prospective purchase, spend time just quietly observing them. Usually the most outgoing or aggressive puppy is your best bet. However, do not overlook the more reserved puppy. Most dogs are wary of strangers, so reserve may indicate caution, not timidity. He may calmly accept your presence when he senses that all is well. In any event, never force yourself on a puppy—let him come to you. Beware of the puppy that hides in the corner and won't emerge until you have left. Chances are he will always be high-strung and may develop more undesirable habits as a result of his nervousness.

Because at least three out of four prospective purchasers of dogs want to buy a young rather than an adult or almost adult dog, the problem of preparing for the arrival of a permanent canine house guest almost always means preparing for the arrival of a puppy. This is not to say that there is anything wrong with purchasing an adult dog; on the contrary, such a purchase has definite advantages in that it often allows freedom from housebreaking chores and rigorous feeding schedules, and these are a definite benefit to prospective purchasers who have little time to spare. Since the great majority of dog buyers, however, prefer to watch their pet grow from sprawlingly playful puppyhood to dignified maturity, buying a dog, practically speaking, means buying a puppy. Before you get a puppy be sure that you are willing to take the responsibility of training him and caring for his physical needs. His early training is most important, as an adult dog that is a well-behaved member of the family is the end product of your early training. Remember that your new puppy knows only

Four-week-old Ibizan puppies at the Ibizans of Islesboro Kennels in Maine. Notice the prominent, characteristic red lozenge (diamond-shaped) spot between the ears even at this tender age.

a life of romping with his littermates and the security of being with his mother, and that coming into your home is a new and sometimes frightening experience for him. He will adjust quickly if you are patient with him and show him what you expect of him. If there are small children in the family be sure that they do not abuse him or play roughly with him. A puppy plays hard, but he also requires frequent periods of rest. Before he comes, decide where he is to sleep and where he is to eat. If your puppy does not have a collar, find out the size he requires and buy an inexpensive one, as he will soon outgrow it. Have the proper grooming equipment on hand. Consult the person from whom you bought the puppy as to the proper food for your puppy, and learn the feeding time and amount that he eats a day. Buy him some toys—usually the breeder will give you some particular toy or toys which he has cherished as a puppy to add to his new ones and to make him less homesick. Get everything you need from your pet shop before you bring the puppy home.

MALE OR FEMALE?

Before buying your puppy you should have made a decision as to whether you want a male or female. Unless you want to breed your pet and raise a litter of puppies, your preference as to the sex of your puppy is strictly a personal choice. On the whole both sexes are pretty much the same in disposition and character, and both make equally good pets.

40

SHOW DOG OR PET?

It is well to define in your own mind the purpose for which you want a dog, and to convey this to the breeder. A great deal of disappointment and dissatisfaction can be avoided by a meeting of the minds between seller and buyer.

Although every well-bred healthy member of the breed makes an ideal companion and pet, actual pet stock is usually the least expensive of the purebred registered stock. The person who asks for a pet, pays a pet-geared price for the animal. Pet stock is least expensive because these dogs are deemed unsuitable for breeding or exhibition in comparison to the standard of perfection for the breed. Generally only skilled breeders and judges can point out the structural differences between a pet and show quality dog.

If you are planning to show your dog, make this clear to the breeder and he will aid you in selecting the best possible specimen of the breed. A show quality dog may be more expensive than one meant for a pet, but it will be able to stand up to show ring competition.

Even though Ibizans originated in the warm climate of the Mediterranean, they also thrive in cold weather, and they love the snow! Photographed here is Treybeau's Melvin, chasing some of his kennel mates. Notice the large outdoor run that becomes necessary when one owns coursing hounds such as the Ibizans.

WHERE TO BUY YOUR IBIZAN HOUND PUPPY

Once you have decided on the particular breed that you want for your pet, your task is to find that one special dog from among several outlets. Buying a well-bred, healthy dog is your foremost concern. By doing a little research in the various dog magazines and newspapers you can locate the names and addresses of breeders and kennels in your area that are known for breeding quality animals. The American Kennel Club will also furnish you with addresses of people to contact that are knowledgeable about your chosen breed.

Your local pet shop, although necessarily restricted from carrying all breeds in stock, may sometimes be able to supply quality puppies on demand. Due to the exorbitant amount of space and time needed to properly rear puppies, pet shops generally prefer to assist owners by supplying all the tools and equipment needed in the raising and training of the puppies. The pet shop proprietor, if unable to obtain a dog for you, can often refer you to a reputable kennel with which he has done business before.

Treybeau's Racing Stripe at 10-weeks-old shows all of the alert intelligence charcteristic of the breed. Notice the upright position of the ears even at this young age.

Bobbee Preu and three nine-week-old puppies which represent the fifth generation of Ibizan breeding in the U.S. The dam was Hathor and their sire Malchus V. Photographed in 1967.

SIGNS OF GOOD HEALTH

Picking out a healthy, attractive little fellow to join the family circle is a different matter from picking a show dog: it is also a great deal less complicated. Often the puppy will pick you. If he does, and it is mutual admiration at first sight, he is the best puppy for you. Trust your eyes and hands to tell if the puppy is sound in body and temperament. Ears and eyes should not have suspicious discharges. Legs should have strong bones; bodies should have solid muscles. Coats should be clean. Lift the hair to see that the skin is free of scales and parasites.

Reliable breeders and pet shops will urge you to take your puppy to the veterinarian of your choice to have the puppy's health checked, and will allow you at least two days to have it done. It should be clearly understood whether rejection by a veterinarian for health reasons means that you have the choice of another puppy from that litter or that you get your money back. Be sure to get the details of this policy before you purchase any puppy.

PAPERS

When you buy a purebred dog you should receive his American Kennel Club registration certificate (or an application form to fill out), a pedigree and a health certificate made out by the breeder's veterinarian.

43

Ready for the race! Reina, Phoenecia and Melvin waiting to be slipped at the first Continental Invitational Lure Coursing event held in the United States. All of these Ibizan Hounds were to become field champions. Each of them courses with a blanket bearing its own "color."

The registration certificate is the official A.K.C. paper. If the puppy was named and registered by his breeder you will want to complete the transfer and send it, with the appropriate fee, to the American Kennel Club. They will transfer the dog to your ownership in their records and send you a new certificate. If you receive, instead, an application for registration, you should fill it out choosing a name for your dog, and mail it, with the fee, to the A.K.C.

The pedigree is a chart showing your puppy's ancestry and is not a part of his official papers. The health certificate will tell what shots have been given and when the next ones are due. Your veterinarian will be appreciative of this information, and will continue with the same series of shots, if they have not been completed. The health certificate will also give the date on which the puppy has been wormed.

Grooming-table training should start while pups are young. Nan Kilgore Koppel sets up a 12-week-old pup for grooming in the ideal show stance. Below: O'Bre-Ons Ospray of Amaris winning Best in Sweepstakes at eight weeks of age at the Ibizan Hound Club of the U.S. East Coast show.

Gena, owned by Kurt Kroll, of Hawthorne, NJ, poses for the camera in this charming photo.

YOUR PUPPY'S BED

Every dog likes to have a place that is his alone. He holds nothing more sacred than his own bed whether it be a rug, dog crate, or dog bed. If you get your puppy a bed be sure to get one which discourages chewing. Also be sure that the bed is large enough to be comfortable for him when he is full grown. Locate it away from drafts and radiators. A word might be said here in defense of the crate, which many pet owners think is cruel and confining. Given a choice, a young dog instinctively selects a secure place in which to lounge, rest or sleep. The walls and ceiling of a crate, even a wire one, answer that need. Once he regards his crate as a safe and reassuring place to stay, you will be able to leave him alone in the house.

FEEDING YOUR IBIZAN HOUND PUPPY

At the time of purchase, most breeders will give you food for a few days, along with instructions for feeding so that your puppy will have the same diet he is accustomed to until you can buy a supply at your pet shop.

As a general rule, a puppy from weaning time (six weeks) to three months of age should be fed four meals a day; from three months to six months, three meals; from six months to one year, two meals. After a year, a dog does well on one meal daily. There are as many feeding schedules as there are breeders, and puppies do fine on all of them, so it is best for the new owner to follow the one given him by the breeder of his puppy. Remember that all dogs are individuals. The amount that will keep your dog in good health is right for him, not the "rule book"

Kathy O'Brien photographed in 1978 with nine-month-old Sylvan Willow of O'Bre-On, O'Bre-Ons Toucan of Sangabar and three-year-old Kreskin Kharisma of O'Bre-On, C.D. To foster pups like Willow and Toucan to a healthy adulthood, the pups' owner must adhere to a schedule of regular and nutritious feedings, and a well-thought-out exercise regimen. As well, it takes plenty of love and attention to make your Ibizan a happy member of the household.

amount. A feeding schedule to give you some idea of what the average puppy will eat is as follows:

Morning meal: Puppy meal with milk.

Afternoon meal: Meat mixed with puppy meal, plus a vitamin-mineral supplement.

Evening meal: Same as afternoon meal, but without a vitamin-mineral supplement.

Do not change the amounts in your puppy's diet too rapidly. If he gets diarrhea it may be that he is eating too much, so cut back on his food and when he is normal again increase his food more slowly.

There is a canned food made especially for puppies which you can buy with a veterinarian's prescription, and several commercially prepared products. Some breeders use this method very successfully from weaning to three months.

TRANSITIONAL DIET

Changing over to an adult program of feeding is not difficult. Very often the puppy will change himself: that is, he will refuse to eat some of his meals. He'll adjust to his one meal (or two meals) a day without any trouble at all.

BREAKING TO COLLAR AND LEASH

Puppies are usually broken to a collar before you bring them home, but even if yours has never worn one it is a simple matter to get him used to it. Put a loose collar on him for a few hours. At first he may scratch at it and try to get it off, but gradually he will take it as a matter of course. To break him to a lead, attach his leash to his collar and let him drag it around. When he becomes used to it pick it up and gently pull him in the direction you want him to go. He will think it is a game, and with a bit of patience on your part he will allow himself to be led.

DISCIPLINING YOUR IBIZAN HOUND PUPPY

The way to have a well-mannered adult dog is to give him firm basic training while he is a puppy. When you say "No" you must mean "No." Your dog will respect you only if you are firm. A six-to eight-week-old puppy is old enough to understand what "No" means. The first time you see your puppy doing something he shouldn't be doing, chewing something he shouldn't chew or wandering in a forbidden area, it's time to teach him. Say "No" firmly. Usually a firm "No" in a disapproving tone of voice is enough to correct your dog, but occasionally you get a puppy that requires a firmer hand, especially as he grows older. In this case hold your puppy firmly and slap him gently across the hindquarters. If this seems cruel, you should realize that no dog resents being disciplined if he is caught in the act of doing something wrong, and your puppy will be intelligent enough to know what the slap was for.

After you have slapped him and you can see that he has learned his lesson, call him to you and talk to him in a pleasant tone of voice—praise him for coming to you. This sounds contradictory, but it works with a puppy. He immediately forgives you, practically tells you that it was his fault and that he deserved his punishment, and promises that it will not happen again. This form of discipline works best and may be used for all misbehaviors.

Never punish your puppy by chasing him around, making occasional swipes with a rolled-up newspaper: punish him only when you have a firm hold on him. Above all, never punish your dog after having called him to you. He must learn to associate coming to you with something pleasant.

48

HOUSEBREAKING

While housebreaking your puppy, do not let him have the run of the house. If you do you will find that he will pick out his own bathroom, which may be in your bedroom or in the middle of the living room rug. Keep him confined to a small area where you can watch him, and you will be able to train him much more easily and speedily. A puppy does not want to dirty his bed, but he does need to be taught where he should go. Spread papers over his living quarters, then watch him carefully. When you notice him starting to whimper, sniff the floor or run agitatedly in little circles, rush him to the place that you want to serve as his relief area and gently hold him there until he relieves himself. Then praise him lavishly. When you remove the soiled papers, leave a small damp piece so that the puppy's sense of smell will lead him back there next time. If he makes a mistake, wash the area at once with warm water, followed by a rinse with water and vinegar or sudsy ammonia. This will kill the odor and prevent discoloration. It shouldn't take more than a few days for him to get the idea of using newspapers. When he becomes fairly consistent, reduce the area of paper to a few sheets in a corner. As soon as you think he has the idea fixed in his mind, you can let him roam around the house a bit, but keep an eye on him. It might be best to keep him on a leash the first few days so that you can rush him back to his paper at any signs of an approaching accident.

The normal healthy puppy will want to relieve himself when he wakes up in the morning, after each feeding and after strenuous exercise. During early puppyhood any excitement, such as the return home of a member of the family or the approach of a visitor, may result in floor-wetting, but that phase should pass in a few weeks. Keep in mind that you can't expect too much from your puppy until he is about five months old. Before that, his muscles and digestive system just aren't under his control.

OUTDOOR HOUSEBREAKING

You can begin outdoor training on a leash even while you are paper-training your puppy. First thing in the morning take him outdoors (to the curb, if you are in the city) and walk him back and forth in a small area until he relieves himself. He will probably make a puddle and then walk around, uncertain of what is expected of him. You can try standing him over a newspaper, which may give him the idea. Praise your dog every time taking him outside brings results, and he will get the idea. You'll find, when you begin the outdoor training, that the male puppy usually requires a longer walk than the female. Both male and female puppies will squat. It isn't until he is older that the male dog will begin to lift his

49

leg. If you hate to give up your sleep, you can train your puppy to go outdoors during the day and use the paper at night.

ALL DOGS NEED TO CHEW

Puppies and young dogs need something with resistance to chew on while their teeth and jaws are developing—for cutting the puppy teeth, to induce growth of the permanent teeth under the puppy teeth, to assist in getting rid of the puppy teeth at the proper time, to help the permanent teeth through the gums, to assure normal jaw development and to settle the permanent teeth solidly in the jaws.

The adult dog's desire to chew stems from the instinct for tooth cleaning, gum massage and jaw exercise—plus the need for an outlet for periodic doggie tensions.

Dental caries as it affects the teeth of humans is virtually unknown in dogs—but tartar accumulates on the teeth of dogs, particularly at the gum line, more rapidly than on the teeth of humans. These accumulations, if not removed, bring irritation, and then infection which erodes the tooth enamel and ultimately destroys the teeth at the roots. Most chewing by adult dogs is an effort to do something about this problem for themselves.

Tooth and jaw development will normally continue until the dog is more than a year old—but sometimes much longer, depending upon the breed, chewing exercise, the rate at which calcium can be utilized and many other factors, known and unknown, which affect the development of individual dogs. Diseases, like distemper for example, may sometimes arrest development of the teeth and jaws, which may resume months, or even years later.

This is why dogs, especially puppies and young dogs, will often destroy property worth hundreds of dollars, when their chewing instinct is not diverted from their owner's possessions, particularly during the widely varying critical period for young dogs.

Saving your possessions from destruction, assuring proper development of teeth and jaws, providing for 'interim' tooth cleaning and gum massage, and channeling doggie tensions into a non-destructive outlet are, therefore, all dependent upon the dog having something suitable for chewing readily available when his instinct tells him to chew. If your purposes, and those of your dog, are to be accomplished, what you provide for chewing must be desirable from the doggie viewpoint, have the necessary functional qualities, and above all, be safe for your dog.

It is very important that dogs not be permitted to chew on anything they can break, or indigestible things from which they can bite sizeable chunks. Sharp pieces, from such as a bone which can be broken by a dog, may pierce the intestine wall and kill. Indigestible things which can be

Nylabone®, a unique 100 percent nylon chew bone, is the perfect chewing pacifier for young dogs in their teething stage, or even for older dogs to help satisfy that occasional urge to chew. Unlike many other dog bones on the market today, Nylabone® does not splinter or fall apart. It will last indefinitely and as it is used it frills, becoming a doggie toothbrush that cleans teeth and massages gums.

bitten off in chunks, such as toys made of rubber compound or cheap plastic, may cause an intestinal stoppage, if not regurgitated—to bring painful death, unless surgery is promptly performed.

Strong natural bones, such as 4 to 8 inch lengths of round shin bone from mature beef—either the kind you can get from your butcher or one of the variety available commercially in pet stores—may serve your dog's teething needs, if his mouth is large enough to handle them effectively.

You may be tempted to give your puppy a smaller bone and he may not be able to break it when you do—but puppies grow rapidly and the power of their jaws constantly increases until maturity. This means that a growing dog may break one of the smaller bones at any time, swallow the pieces and die painfully before you realize what is wrong.

Many people make the mistake of thinking of their dog's teeth in terms of the teeth of the wild carnivores or those of the dog in antiquity. The teeth of the wild carnivorous animals, and the teeth found in the fossils of the dog-like creatures of antiquity, have far thicker and stronger enamel than those of our contemporary dogs.

All hard natural bones are highly abrasive. If your dog is an avid chewer, natural bones may wear away his teeth prematurely; hence, they then should be taken away from your dog when the teething purposes have been served. The badly worn, and usually painful, teeth of many mature dogs can be traced to excessive chewing on natural bones.

Contrary to popular belief, knuckle bones which can be chewed up and swallowed by the dog provide little, if any, useable calcium or other nutriment. They do, however, disturb the digestion of most dogs and cause them to vomit the nourishing food they need.

An old leather shoe is another popular answer to the chewing need—but be very sure that the rubber heel, all nails, and other metal parts such as lace grommets, metal arches, etc., have been removed. Be especially careful to get all of the nails. A chunk of rubber heel can cause an intestinal stoppage. If it has a nail in it, the intestine wall may be pierced or torn. Then there is, of course, always the hazard that your dog may fail to differentiate between his shoe and yours, and eat up a good pair while you're not looking.

Dried rawhide products of various types, shapes, sizes and prices have come on the market during the past few years. They don't serve the primary chewing functions very well, they are a bit messy when wet from mouthing, and most dogs chew them up rather rapidly—but they have been considered safe for dogs until recently. During the past few months, however, a number of cases of death, and near death, by strangulation have been reported to be the result of partially swallowed chunks of rawhide swelling in the throat. More recently, some veterinarians have been attributing cases of acute constipation to large pieces of incompletely digested rawhide in the intestine.

The nylon bones, especially those with natural meat and bone fractions added, are probably the most complete, safe and economical answer to the chewing need. Dogs cannot break them or bite off sizeable chunks; hence, they are completely safe—and being longer lasting than other things offered for the purpose, they are economical.

Hard chewing raises little bristle-like projections on the surface of the nylon bones—to provide effective interim tooth cleaning and vigorous gum massage, much in the same way your tooth brush does it for you. The little projections are raked off and swallowed in the form of thin shavings—but the chemistry of the nylon is such that they break down in the stomach fluids and pass through without effect.

The toughness of the nylon provides the strong chewing resistance needed for important jaw exercise and effective help for the teething functions—but there is no tooth wear because nylon is non-abrasive. Being inert, nylon does not support the growth of microorganisms—and it can be washed in soap and water, or it can be sterilized by boiling or in an autoclave.

Nylabone® is highly recommended by veterinarians as a safe, healthy nylon bone that can't splinter or chip. Instead, Nylabone is frizzled by the dog's chewing action, creating a toothbrush-like surface that cleanses the teeth and massages the gums. Nylabone® and Nylaball®, the only chew products made of flavor-impregnated solid nylon, are available in your local pet shop.

Nothing, however, substitutes for periodic professional attention to your dog's teeth and gums, not any more than your toothbrush can do that for you. Have your dog's teeth cleaned by your veterinarian at least once a year, twice a year is better—and he will be healthier, happier and far more pleasant to live with.

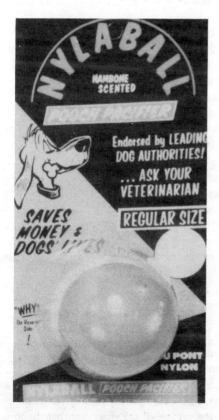

Nylaball®, another fully nylon dog pacifier, is a hygienic chew product that will hold your dog's interest for hours. Impregnated with ham flavor, it is a wholly safe, long-lasting product that cannot endanger your dog's life with the threat of fragments that may become lodged in his throat.

5. OBEDIENCE TRAINING

WHEN TO START TRAINING

You should never begin *serious* obedience training before your dog is seven or eight months old. (Some animal psychologists state that puppies can begin training when seven weeks old, if certain techniques are followed. These techniques, however, are still experimental and should be left to the professional trainer.) While your dog is still in his early puppyhood, concentrate on winning his confidence so he will love and admire you. Basic training can be started at the age of three or four months. He should be taught to walk nicely on a leash, sit and lie down on command, and come when he is called.

YOUR PART IN TRAINING

You must patiently demonstrate to your dog what each word of command means. Guide him with your hands and the training leash, reassuring him with your voice, through whatever routine you are teaching him. Repeat the word associated with the act. Demonstrate again and again to give the dog a chance to make the connection in his mind.

Once he begins to get the idea, use the word of command without any physical guidance. Drill him. When he makes mistakes, correct him, kindly at first, more severely as his training progresses. Try not to lose your patience or become irritated, and never slap him with your hand or the leash during the training session. Withholding praise or rebuking him will make him feel bad enough.

When he does what you want, praise him lavishly with words and with pats. Don't continually reward with dog candy or treats in training. The dog that gets into the habit of performing for a treat will seldom be fully dependable when he can't smell or see one in the offing. When he carries out a command, even though his performance is slow or sloppy, praise him and he will perform more readily the next time.

THE TRAINING VOICE

When you start training your dog, use your training voice, giving commands in a firm, clear tone. Once you give a command, persist until it is obeyed, even if you have to pull the dog to obey you. He must learn that training is different from playing, that a command once given must be obeyed no matter what distractions are present. Remember that the tone and pitch of your voice, not loudness, are the qualities that will influence your dog most.

Be consistent in the use of words during training. Confine your commands to as few words as possible and never change them. It is best for only one person to carry on the dog's training, because different people will use different words and tactics that will confuse your dog. The dog who hears "come," "get over here," "hurry up," "here, Rex," and other commands when he is wanted will become totally confused.

TRAINING LESSONS

Training is hard on the dog and the trainer. A young dog just cannot take more than ten minutes of training at a stretch, so limit the length of your first lessons. Then you can gradually increase the length of time to about thirty minutes. You'll find that you too will tend to become impatient when you stretch out a training lesson. If you find yourself losing your temper, stop and resume the lesson at another time. Before and after each lesson have a play period, but don't play during a training session. Even the youngest dog soon learns that schooling is a serious matter; fun comes afterward.

Don't spend too much time on one phase of training, or the dog will become bored. Always try to end a lesson on a pleasant note. Actually, in nine cases out of ten, if your dog isn't doing what you want it's because you're not getting the idea over to him properly.

YOUR TRAINING EQUIPMENT AND ITS USE

The leash is more properly called the lead, so we'll use that term here. The best leads for training are the six-foot webbed-cloth leads, usually olive-drab in color, and the six-foot leather lead. Fancier leads are available and may be used if desired.

You'll need a metal-link collar, called a choke chain, consisting of a metal chain with rings on each end. Even though the name may sound frightening, it won't hurt your dog, and it is an absolute MUST in training. There is a right and a wrong way to put the training collar on. It should go around the dog's neck so that you can attach the lead to the ring at the end of the chain which passes over, not under the neck. It is most important that the collar is put on properly so it will tighten when the lead is pulled and ease when you relax your grip.

The correct way to hold the lead is also very important, as the collar should have some slack in it at all times, except when correcting. Holding the loop in your right hand, extend your arm out to the side, even with your shoulder. With your left hand, grasp the lead as close as possible to the collar, without making it tight. The remaining portion of the lead can

Your local pet store is the source of a large selection of leads and collars that can be used for training or showing, or just taking your pet for a walk. Since puppies quickly outgrow their first collars and leads, plan to purchase at least two sets of equipment.

be made into a loop which is held in the right hand. Keep this arm close to your body. Most corrections will be made with the left hand by giving the lead a jerk in the direction you want the dog to go.

HEELING

"Heeling" in dog language means having your dog walk alongside you on your left side, close to your leg, on lead or off. With patience and effort you can train your dog to walk with you even on a crowded street or in the presence of other dogs.

Now that you have learned the correct way to put on your dog's collar and how to hold the lead, you are ready to start with his first lesson in heeling. Make the dog sit at your left side. Using the dog's name and the command "Heel," start forward on your LEFT foot, giving a tug on the lead to get the dog started. Always use the dog's name first, followed by the command, such as "Rex, heel." Saying his name will help get his attention and will let him know that you are about to give a command.

Walk briskly, with even steps, going around in a large circle, square or straight line. While walking, make sure that your dog stays on the left side and close to your leg. If he lags behind, snap gently on the lead to get him up to you, then praise him lavishly for doing well. If he forges ahead or swings wide, stop and jerk the lead sharply and bring him back to the proper position. Always praise him when he returns to the correct place. As soon as you have snapped the lead to correct your dog, let it go slack again at the desired length. Don't drag the dog or keep the lead taut as this will develop into a tug of war which is ineffective.

To keep your dog's attention, talk to him as you keep him in place. You can also do a series of fast about-turns, giving the lead a jerk as you turn. He will gradually learn that he must pay attention or be jerked to your side. You can vary the routine by changing speeds, doing turns, figure-eights, and by zig-zagging across the training area.

"HEEL" MEANS "SIT," TOO

To the dog, the command "Heel" will also mean that he has to sit in the heel position at your left side when you stop walking with no additional command from you. As you practice heeling, make him sit whenever you stop, at first using the word "Sit," then with no command at all. He'll soon get the idea and sit down when you stop and wait for the command "Heel" to start walking again.

TRAINING TO SIT

Training your dog to sit should be fairly easy. Stand him on your left side, holding the lead fairly short, and command him to "Sit." As you give the verbal command, pull up slightly with the lead and push his hindquarters down. Do not let him lie down or stand up. If he does lie down, snap up on the lead until he rises to a sitting position again. If he is slow to respond, tug more sharply until he has done what you want him to. Keep him in a sitting position for a moment, then release the pressure on the lead and praise him. Constantly repeat the command as you hold him in a sitting position, thus fitting the word to the action in his mind. If he moves at all, immediately repeat the command and press him into a sitting position. After a time he will begin to get the idea and will sit without having to push his hindquarters down. When he reaches that stage, insist that he sit on command. Praise him often, always rewarding a correct action with your praise and affection.

THE "LIE DOWN" OR "DOWN"

The object of this is to get the dog to lie down either on the verbal command "Down" or when you give the hand signal, your hand raised in front of you, palm down. However, until the dog is really sure of the meaning of the command, and will do it by himself with no forcible action from you, the hand signal should only be used to accompany the verbal command. This command may be more difficult at first because it places the dog in a defenseless position, which may cause him to bolt away. Be lavish with your praise and affection when he has assumed the correct position and he will soon learn that nothing bad happens to him, and on the contrary will associate the "Down" position with pleasing his master or mistress.

Don't start training to lie down until the dog is almost letter-perfect in sitting on command. Place the dog in a sit, and kneel before him. With both hands, reach forward to his legs and take one front leg in each hand, thumbs up, holding just above the elbows. Lift his legs slightly off the ground and pull them somewhat out in front of him. Simultaneously, give the command "Down" and lower his front legs to the ground.

Hold the dog down and stroke him to let him know that staying down is what you want him to do. This method is far better than forcing a young dog down. Using force can cause him to become very frightened and he will begin to dislike any training. Always talk to your dog and let him know that you are very pleased with him, and soon you will find that you have a happy working dog.

After he begins to get the idea, slide the lead under your left foot and give the command "Down." At the same time, pull the lead. This will help get the dog down. Meanwhile, raise your hand in the down signal. Don't expect to accomplish all this in one session. Be patient and work with the dog. He'll cooperate if you show him just what you expect him to do.

THE "STAY"

The next step is to train your dog to stay either in a "Sit" or "Down" position. As before, use the lead to teach this command until your dog is responding perfectly to your instruction, then you may try it off the lead. To begin with the Sit-Stay, place your dog in a sitting position beside you in the automatic heel-sit position. Holding the leash in one hand (most trainers prefer the left), take a long step forward and turn to face him holding your free hand open, palm toward him, fingers pointing downward, in front of his nose and speak the command "Stay." If he offers to follow you, as it would be natural for him to do since this has been his ready position for heel, snap up on the lead to return him to the sit, put your hand in front of his face and repeat the command firmly once more. Allow him to remain sitting for a few seconds before going through the procedure again. Each time he successfully performs, praise him profusely and show him you are pleased with him.

Repeat this procedure until your dog behaves as if he understands what is expected of him. When he has mastered this procedure, step away to the right of him, then behind, then a few steps forward, a few steps to the side, and so on, until you have gone the full length of the leash. Anytime your dog offers to follow you, snap upward on the leash, extending your arm palm forward to him and repeat the command sharply. When he has demonstrated a willingness to remain in the correct position while you walk the full extent of the lead, you are ready to train him to remain in position using a longer length of cord, about 25 or 30 feet, and finally the Sit-Stay off the lead.

Once the Sit-Stay is learned, you can teach the Down-Stay by beginning with the Down command, then apply approximately the same methods as in the Sit-Stay.

THE COME ON COMMAND

You can train your dog to come when you call him if you begin when he is young. At first, work with him on lead. Sit the dog, then back away the length of the lead and call him, putting into your voice as much coaxing affection as possible. Give an easy tug on the lead to get him started. When he does come, make a big fuss over him—it might help at this point to give him a small piece of dog candy or food as a reward. He should get the idea soon. You can also move away from him the full length of the lead and call to him something like "Rex, come," then run backward a few steps and stop, making him sit directly in front of you.

Don't be too eager to practice coming on command off lead. Wait until you are certain that you have the dog under perfect control before you try calling him when he's free. Once he gets the idea that he can disobey a command and get away with it, your training program will suffer a serious setback. Keep in mind that your dog's life may depend on his immediate response to a command to come when he is called. If he disobeys off lead, put the lead back on and correct him severely with jerks of the lead.

TEACHING TO COME TO HEEL

The object of this is for you to stand still, say "Heel," and have your dog come right over to you and sit by your left knee in the heel position. If your dog has been trained to sit without command every time you stop, he's ready for this step.

Sit him in front of and facing you and step back one step. Moving only your left foot, pull the dog behind you, then step forward and pull him around until he is in a heel position. You can also have the dog go around by passing the lead behind your back. Use your left heel to straighten him out if he begins to sit behind you or crookedly. This may take a little work, but he will get the idea if you show him just what you want.

THE STAND

Your dog should be trained to stand in one spot without moving his feet, and he should allow a stranger to run his hand over his body and legs without showing any resentment or fear. Employ the same method you used in training him to stay on the sit and down. While walking, place your left hand out, palm toward his nose, and command him to stay. His first impulse will be to sit, so be prepared to stop him by placing your hand under his body, near his hindquarters, and holding him until he gets the idea that this is different from the command to sit. Praise him for standing, then walk to the end of the lead. Correct him strongly if he starts to move. Have a stranger approach him and run his hands over the dog's back and down his legs. Keep him standing until you come back to him. Walk around him from his left side, come to the heel position, and make sure that he does not sit until you command him to. This is a very valuable exercise. If you plan to show your dog, he will have to learn to stand in a show pose and allow the judge to examine him. The judge will run his hands along the dog's back and down the legs, so it is important that the dog stands calmly and steadfastly.

TRAINING SCHOOLS AND CLASSES

There are dog training schools in all parts of the country, some sponsored by the local humane society.

If you feel that you lack the time or the skill to train your dog yourself, there are professional dog trainers who will do it for you, but basically dog training is a matter of training YOU and your dog to work together as a team, and if you don't do it yourself you will miss a lot of fun. Don't give up after trying unsuccessfully for a short time. Try a little harder and you and your dog will be able to work things out.

ADVANCED TRAINING AND OBEDIENCE TRIALS

Once you begin training your dog and you see how well he does, you'll probably be bitten by the "obedience bug"—the desire to enter him in obedience trials held under American Kennel Club auspices.

The A.K.C. obedience trials are divided into three classes: Novice, Open and Utility.

In trials for advanced obedience degrees, your dog will have to successfully accomplish two scent discrimination exercises. From among several objects like the ones above, he will have to choose the one that has been touched by his handler or owner and carries that person's scent.

In the Novice Class the dog will be judged on the following basis:

TEST MAXIMUM SCORE

Test	Maximum Score
Heel on lead	40
Stand for examination	30
Heel free—off lead	40
Recall (come on command)	30
One-minute sit (handler in ring)	30
Three-minute down (handler in ring)	30
Maximum total score	200

If the dog "qualifies" in three shows by earning at least 50% of the points for each test, with a total of at least 170 for the trial, he has earned the Companion Dog degree and the letters C.D. (Companion Dog) are entered after his name in the American Kennel Club records.

The hurdle is used in different events in advanced obedience competition. It figures in the single jump, in the retrieve, and in the directed jump. The bar is adjustable, so that the height a dog must jump to successfully accomplish the particular exercise will be proportional to his size. Informal hurdles can be simulated out of a variety of different items for backyard or indoor practice before the actual trial.

After the dog has earned his Companion Dog title, he is eligible to enter the Open Class competition and compete for his next degree. He will be judged on this basis:

TEST MAXIMUM SCORE

Heel free	40
Drop on recall	30
Retrieve (wooden dumbbell) on flat	20
Retrieve over obstacle (hurdle)	30
Broad jump	20
Three-minute sit (handler out of ring)	30
Five-minute down (handler out of ring)	30
Maximum total score	200

Again he must qualify in three shows for the C.D.X. (Companion Dog Excellent) title, earning at least 50% of the points for each test, with a total of at least 170 for the trial. He is then eligible to compete in the Utility Class, where he can earn the Utility Dog (U.D.) degree in these rugged tests:

TEST MAXIMUM SCORE

Scent discrimination (picking up article handled by master from group) Article 1	30
Scent discrimination Article 2	30
Directed Retrieve	30
Signal exercise (heeling, etc., on hand signal)	40
Directed jumping (over hurdle and bar jump)	40
Group examination	30
Maximum total score	200

For more complete information about these obedience trials, write for the American Kennel Club's *Regulations and Standards for Obedience Trials*. Dogs that are disqualified from breed shows because of neutering or physical defects are eligible to compete in these trials. Besides the formal A.K.C. obedience trials, there are informal "match" trials in which dogs compete for ribbons and inexpensive trophies. These shows are run by many local fanciers' clubs and by all-breed obedience clubs. In many localities the humane society and other groups conduct their own obedience shows. Your local newspaper, pet shop proprietor or kennel club can keep you informed about such shows in your vicinity, and you will find them listed in the different dog magazines or in the pet column of your paper.

6. BREEDING YOUR DOG

THE QUESTION OF SPAYING

If you feel that you will never want to raise a litter of purebred puppies, and if you do not wish to risk the possibility of an undesirable mating and surplus mongrel puppies inevitably destined for euthanasia at the local pound, you may want to have your female spayed. Spaying is generally best performed after the female has passed her first heat and before her first birthday; this allows the female to attain the normal female characteristics, while still being young enough to avoid the possible complications encountered when an older female is spayed. A spayed female will remain a healthy, lively pet. You often hear that an altered female will become very fat. However, if you cut down on her food intake, she will not gain weight.

On the other hand, if you wish to show your dog in American Kennel Club competition (altered females are disqualified) or enjoy the excitement and feeling of accomplishment of breeding and raising a litter of quality puppies, particularly in your breed and from your pet, then do not spay your dog until a more appropriate time.

Male dogs are almost never altered (castrated) unless they exhibit excessive sexual tendencies.

SEXUAL PHYSIOLOGY

Females usually reach sexual maturity (indicated by the first heat cycle, or season) at eight or nine months of age, but sexual maturity may occur as early as six months or as late as thirteen months of age. Generally, the larger the breed is the longer it takes to reach full maturity.

The average heat cycle (estrus period) lasts for twenty or twenty-one days, and occurs approximately every six months. For about five days immediately preceeding the heat period, the female generally displays restlessness and an increased appetite. The vulva, or external genitals, begins to swell. The discharge, which is bright red at the onset and gradually becomes pale pink to straw in color, increases in quantity for several days and then slowly subsides, finally ceasing altogether. The vaginal discharge is subject to much variation; in some bitches it is quite heavy, in others it may never appear, and in some it may be so slight as to go unnoticed.

About eight or nine days after the first appearance of the discharge, the female becomes very playful with other dogs, but will not allow a mating

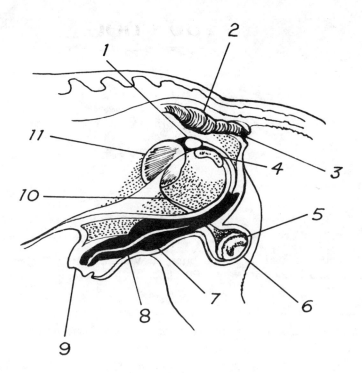

Reproductive system of a male dog: 1. Prostate 2. Rectum 3. Anus 4. Section of pelvic bone 5. Testicle 6. Scrotum 7. Bulb (part of Penis) 8. Penis 9. Sheath 10. Vas deferens 11. Bladder.

to take place. Anywhere from the tenth or eleventh day to the seventeenth or eighteenth day, the female will accept males and be able to conceive. Many biologists apply the term "heat" only to this receptive phase rather than to the whole estrus period, as is commonly done by dog fanciers.

The ova (egg cells) from the female's ovaries are discharged into the oviduct toward the close of the acceptance phase, usually the sixteenth to eighteenth day. From the eighteenth day until the end of the cycle, the female is still attractive to males, but she will repulse their advances. The entire estrus, however, may be quite variable; in some females vaginal bleeding ends and mating begins on the fourth day; in others the discharge may continue throughout the entire cycle and the female will not accept males until the seventeenth day or even later.

The male dog—simply referred to by fanciers as the "dog" or "stud," in contrast to the female, which is referred to as the "bitch"—upon reaching sexual maturity, usually at about six to eight months, is able,

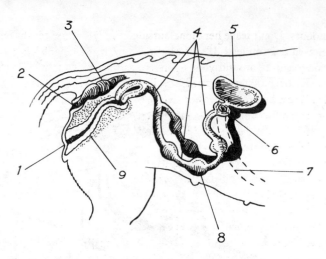

Reproductive system of the bitch: 1. Vulva 2. Anus 3. Rectum 4. Uterus 5. Kidney 6. Ovary 7. Ribs (indicated) 8. Developing embryo 9. Vagina.

like other domesticated mammals, to breed at any time throughout the year.

The testes, the sperm-producing organs of the male, descend from the body cavity into the scrotum at birth. The condition of cryptorchidism refers to the retention of one or both testes within the body cavity. A testicle retained within the body cavity is in an environment too hot for it to function normally. A retained testicle may also become cancerous. If only one testicle descends, the dog is known as a monorchid; if neither descends, the dog is known as an anorchid (dog fanciers, however, refer to a dog with the latter condition as a cryptorchid). A monorchid dog is a fertile animal; an anorchid is sterile.

The male dog's penis has a bulbous enlargement at its base and, in addition, like the penis of a number of other mammals, contains a bone. When mating occurs, pressure on the penis causes a reflex action that fills the bulb with blood, swelling it to five times its normal size within the female. This locks, or ties, the two animals together. After ejaculation, the animals usually remain tied for fifteen to thirty minutes. However, they may separate very quickly or remain together an hour or more, depending on the length of time for the blood to drain from the bulb.

CARE OF THE FEMALE IN ESTRUS

If you have a dog-proof run within your yard, it will be safe to leave your female in season there; if you don't have such a run, she should be shut indoors. Don't leave her alone outside even for a minute; she should be exercised only on lead. If you want to prevent the neighborhood dogs from congregating around your doorstep, as they inevitably will as soon as they discover that your female is in season, take her some distance from the house before you let her relieve herself. Take her in your car to a park or field for a chance to "stretch" her legs (always on lead, of course). Keep watch for male dogs, and if one approaches take the female back to the car. After the three weeks are up you can let her out as before with no worry that she can have puppies until her next season.

Some owners find it simpler to board their female at a kennel until her season is over. However, it really is not difficult to watch your female at home. There are various products on the market which are useful at this time. Although the female in season keeps herself quite clean, sometimes she unavoidably stains furniture or rugs. You can buy sanitary belts made expecially for dogs at your pet shop. Consult your veterinarian for information on pills to be taken to check odor during this period. There also is a pill that prevents the female from coming in season for extended periods, and there are many different types of liquids, powders and sprays of varying efficiency used to keep male dogs away. However, the

There are several products on the market designed to make life easier for both you and your bitch during the estrus cycle. Sanitary pads for dogs are one of these items and come complete with a belt for holding the pad in place.

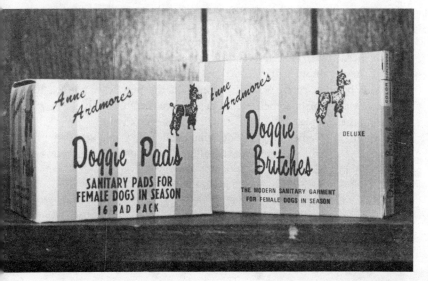

one safe rule (whatever products you use) is: keep your bitch away from dogs that could mount her.

SHOULD YOU BREED YOUR MALE?

Deciding whether or not to use a male dog as a stud is a question with two sides. The arguments for and against using a dog as a stud are often very close to ridiculous. A classic example would be the tale that once you use a dog as a stud he will lose his value as a show dog or any one of the other functions a dog may have. A sound rule may well be: if you have a stud who has proven his worth at the shows, place his services out for hire, if only for the betterment of the breed; if your dog is not of show quality, do not use him as a stud.

Top champion studs can bring their owners many dollars in breeding revenue. If the stud is as good as you feel he is, his services will soon be in great demand. Using a dog as a stud will not lower his value in other functions in any way. Many breeders will permit a male dog to breed an experienced female once, when about a year old, and then they begin to show their stud until he has gained his conformation championship. He is then placed out for hire through advertising in the various bulletins, journals and show catalogues, and through the stud registers maintained by many pet shops and kennel clubs.

SHOULD YOU BREED YOUR FEMALE?

If you are an amateur and decide to breed your female it would be wise to talk with a breeder and find out all that breeding and caring for puppies entails. You must be prepared to assume the responsibility of caring for the mother through her pregnancy and for the puppies until they are of saleable age. Raising a litter of puppies can be a rewarding experience, but it means work as well as fun, and there is no guarantee of financial profit. As the puppies grow older and require more room and care, the amateur breeder, in desperation, often sells the puppies for much less than they are worth; sometimes he has to give them away. If the cost of keeping the puppies will drain your finances, think twice.

If you have given careful consideration to all these things and still want to breed your female, remember that there is some preparation necessary before taking this step.

WHEN TO BREED

It is usually best to breed in the second or third season of your bitch. Consider when the puppies will be born and whether their birth and later care will interfere with your work or vacation plans. Gestation period is approximately fifty-eight to sixty-five days. Allow enough time to select

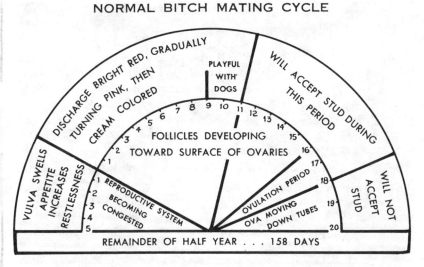

DISCHARGE BRIGHT RED, GRADUALLY TURNING PINK, THEN CREAM COLORED

PLAYFUL WITH DOGS

WILL ACCEPT STUD DURING THIS PERIOD

FOLLICLES DEVELOPING
TOWARD SURFACE OF OVARIES

VULVA SWELLS
APPETITE INCREASES
RESTLESSNESS

REPRODUCTIVE SYSTEM BECOMING CONGESTED

OVULATION PERIOD
OVA MOVING DOWN TUBES

WILL NOT ACCEPT STUD

REMAINDER OF HALF YEAR . . . 158 DAYS

the right stud for her. Don't be in a position of having to settle for any available stud if she comes into season sooner than expected. Your female will probably be ready to breed twelve days after the first colored discharge. You can usually make arrangements to board her with the owner of the male for a few days to insure her being there at the proper time, or you can take her to be mated and bring her home the same day. If she still appears receptive she may be bred again a day or two later. Some females never show signs of willingness, so it helps to have the experience of a breeder. The second day after the discharge changes color is the proper time; she may be bred for about three days following. For an additional week or so she may have some discharge and attract other dogs by her odor, but she can seldom be bred at this time.

HOW TO SELECT A STUD

Choose a mate for your female with an eye to countering her deficiencies. If possible, both male and female should have several ancestors in common within the last two or three generations, as such combinations generally "click" best. The male should have a good show record himself or be the sire of champions. The owner of the stud usually charges a fee for the use of the dog. The fee varies. Payment of a fee does not guarantee a litter, but it does generally confer the right to breed your female again to the stud if she does not have puppies the first time. In some cases the owner of the stud will agree to take a choice puppy in place of the stud fee. You and the owner of the stud should settle all details beforehand, including such questions as what age the puppies should reach before the

Maintenance of a state of excellent health is essential if you are contemplating breeding your bitch or stud. Poor health may not only interfere with reproductive processes but can actually rob your dog of his or her interest in mating. If you are not confident in commercial preparations, consult your vet for the best vitamin supplements to add to your dog's diet.

stud's owner can make his choice, what disposition is made of the single surviving puppy under an agreement by which the stud owner has the pick of the litter, and so on. In all cases, it is best that all agreements entered into by bitch owner and stud owner be in the form of a written contract.

It is customary for the female to be sent to the male. If the stud dog of your choice lives any distance from you, you will have to make arrangements to have your female shipped to him. The quickest way is by air, and if you call your nearest airport the airline people will give you information as to the best and fastest flight. Some airlines furnish their own crates for shipping, whereas others require that you furnish your own. The owner of the stud will make the arrangements for shipping the female back to you. You have to pay all shipping charges.

PREPARATION FOR BREEDING

Before you breed your female, make sure she is in good health. She should be neither too thin nor too fat. Skin diseases must be cured before breeding; a bitch with skin diseases can pass them on to her puppies. If

Perpetual Whelping Chart

	1	2	3	4	5	6	7	8	9	10	11	12	13	14	15	16	17	18	19	20	21	22	23	24	25	26	27	28	29	30	31
Bred—Jan.	1	2	3	4	5	6	7	8	9	10	11	12	13	14	15	16	17	18	19	20	21	22	23	24	25	26	27	28	29	30	31
Due—March	5	6	7	8	9	10	11	12	13	14	15	16	17	18	19	20	21	22	23	24	25	26	27	28	29	30	31	April 1	2	3	4
Bred—Feb.	1	2	3	4	5	6	7	8	9	10	11	12	13	14	15	16	17	18	19	20	21	22	23	24	25	26	27	28			
Due—April	5	6	7	8	9	10	11	12	13	14	15	16	17	18	19	20	21	22	23	24	25	26	27	28	29	30	May 1	2			
Bred—Mar.	1	2	3	4	5	6	7	8	9	10	11	12	13	14	15	16	17	18	19	20	21	22	23	24	25	26	27	28	29	30	31
Due—May	3	4	5	6	7	8	9	10	11	12	13	14	15	16	17	18	19	20	21	22	23	24	25	26	27	28	29	30	31	June 1	2
Bred—Apr.	1	2	3	4	5	6	7	8	9	10	11	12	13	14	15	16	17	18	19	20	21	22	23	24	25	26	27	28	29	30	
Due—June	3	4	5	6	7	8	9	10	11	12	13	14	15	16	17	18	19	20	21	22	23	24	25	26	27	28	29	30	July 1	2	
Bred—May	1	2	3	4	5	6	7	8	9	10	11	12	13	14	15	16	17	18	19	20	21	22	23	24	25	26	27	28	29	30	31
Due—July	3	4	5	6	7	8	9	10	11	12	13	14	15	16	17	18	19	20	21	22	23	24	25	26	27	28	29	30	31	August 1	2
Bred—June	1	2	3	4	5	6	7	8	9	10	11	12	13	14	15	16	17	18	19	20	21	22	23	24	25	26	27	28	29	30	
Due—August	3	4	5	6	7	8	9	10	11	12	13	14	15	16	17	18	19	20	21	22	23	24	25	26	27	28	29	30	31	Sept. 1	
Bred—July	1	2	3	4	5	6	7	8	9	10	11	12	13	14	15	16	17	18	19	20	21	22	23	24	25	26	27	28	29	30	31
Due—September	2	3	4	5	6	7	8	9	10	11	12	13	14	15	16	17	18	19	20	21	22	23	24	25	26	27	28	29	30	Oct. 1	2
Bred—Aug.	1	2	3	4	5	6	7	8	9	10	11	12	13	14	15	16	17	18	19	20	21	22	23	24	25	26	27	28	29	30	31
Due—October	3	4	5	6	7	8	9	10	11	12	13	14	15	16	17	18	19	20	21	22	23	24	25	26	27	28	29	30	31	Nov. 1	2
Bred—Sept.	1	2	3	4	5	6	7	8	9	10	11	12	13	14	15	16	17	18	19	20	21	22	23	24	25	26	27	28	29	30	
Due—November	3	4	5	6	7	8	9	10	11	12	13	14	15	16	17	18	19	20	21	22	23	24	25	26	27	28	29	30	Dec. 1	2	
Bred—Oct.	1	2	3	4	5	6	7	8	9	10	11	12	13	14	15	16	17	18	19	20	21	22	23	24	25	26	27	28	29	30	31
Due—December	3	4	5	6	7	8	9	10	11	12	13	14	15	16	17	18	19	20	21	22	23	24	25	26	27	28	29	30	31	Jan. 1	2
Bred—Nov.	1	2	3	4	5	6	7	8	9	10	11	12	13	14	15	16	17	18	19	20	21	22	23	24	25	26	27	28	29	30	
Due—January	3	4	5	6	7	8	9	10	11	12	13	14	15	16	17	18	19	20	21	22	23	24	25	26	27	28	29	30	31	Feb. 1	
Bred—Dec.	1	2	3	4	5	6	7	8	9	10	11	12	13	14	15	16	17	18	19	20	21	22	23	24	25	26	27	28	29	30	31
Due—February	2	3	4	5	6	7	8	9	10	11	12	13	14	15	16	17	18	19	20	21	22	23	24	25	26	27	28	March 1	2	3	4

she has worms she should be wormed before being bred, or within three weeks afterward. It is a good idea to have your veterinarian give her a booster shot for distemper and hepatitis before the puppies are born. This will increase the immunity the puppies receive during their early, most vulnerable period. Choose a dependable veterinarian and rely on him if there is an emergency when your female whelps.

Do not breed your bitch after she reaches six years of age. If you wish to breed her several times while she is young, it is wise to breed her only once a year. In other words, breed her, skip at least one season, and then breed her again. This will allow her to gain back her full strength between whelpings.

THE IMPORTANCE AND APPLICATION OF GENETICS

Any person attempting to breed dogs should have a basic understanding of the transmission of traits, or characteristics, from the parents to the offspring and some familiarity with the more widely used genetic terms that he will probably encounter. A knowledge of the fundamental mechanics of genetics enables a breeder to better comprehend the passing on of good traits and bad from generation to generation and how a stud and bitch either complement or detract from each other's traits. It enables him to make a more judicial and scientific decision in selecting potential mates.

Inheritance, fundamentally, is due to the existence of microscopic units, known as *GENES,* present in the cells of all individuals. Genes somehow control the biochemical reactions that occur within the embryo or adult organism. This control results in changing or guiding the development of the organism's characteristics. A "string" of attached genes is known as a *CHROMOSOME.* With a few important exceptions, every chromosome has a partner chromosome carrying a duplicate or equivalent set of genes. Each gene, therefore, has a partner gene, known as an *ALLELE.* The number of different pairs of chromosomes present in the cells of the organism varies with the type of organism; a certain parasitic worm has only one pair, a certain fruit fly has four different pairs, man has 23 different pairs and your dog has 39 different pairs per cell. Because each chromosome may have many hundreds of genes, a single cell of the body may contain a total of several thousand genes. Heredity is obviously a very complex matter.

In the simplest form of genetic inheritance, one particular gene and its duplicate, or allele, on the partner chromosome control a single characteristic. The presence of freckles in the human skin, for example, is believed to be due to the influence of a single pair of genes.

Each cell of the body contains the specific number of paired

FERTILIZATION

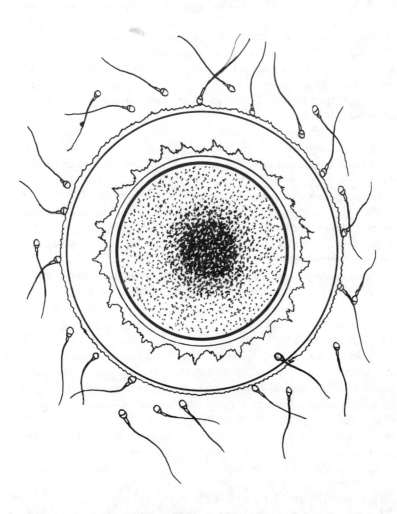

An egg, a special giant cell which the female ovaries produce, is being assaulted by sperm which are attempting to pierce the outer layer of the cell. Only one sperm cell penetration is necessary for fertilization. The first sperm to enter and reach the nucleus will bring with it the necessary chromosomes which will unite with those of the egg. With this union, the full complement of chromosomes necessary for the creation of a new fetus is complete. No other sperm cells are now able to penetrate the egg.

chromosomes characteristic of the organism. Because each type of gene is present on both chromosomes of a chromosome pair, each type of gene is therefore present in duplicate. The fusion of a sperm cell from the male with an egg cell from the female, as occurs in fertilization, should therefore result in offspring having a quadruplicate number (4) of each type of gene. Mating of these individuals would then produce progeny having an octuplicate number (8) of each type of gene, and so on. This, however, is normally prevented by a special process. When ordinary body cells prepare to divide to form more tissue, each pair of chromosomes duplicates itself so that there are four partner chromosomes of each kind instead of only two. When the cell divides, two of the four partners, or one pair, go into each new cell. This process, known as *MITOSIS*, insures that each new body cell contains the proper number of chromosomes. Reproductive cells (sperm and egg cells), however, undergo a special kind of division known as *MEIOSIS*. In meiosis, the chromosome pairs do not duplicate themselves, and thus when the reproductive cells reach the final dividing stage only one chromosome, or one-half of the pair, goes into each new reproductive cell. Each reproductive cell, therefore, has only half the normal number of chromosomes. These are referred to as *HAPLOID* cells, in contrast to *DIPLOID* cells, which have the full number of chromosomes. When the haploid sperm cell fuses with the haploid egg cell in fertilization, the resulting offspring has the normal diploid number of chromosomes.

If both partner genes, or alleles, affect the trait in an identical manner, the genes are said to be *HOMOZYGOUS*, but if one affects the character in a manner different from the other gene, or allele, the genes are said to be *HETEROZYGOUS*. For example, in the pair of genes affecting eye color in humans, if each gene of the pair produces blue eyes, while the other gene, or allele, produces brown eyes, they are said to be heterozygous. The presence of heterozygous genes raises the question, "Will the offspring have blue eyes or brown eyes?" which in turn introduces another genetic principle.

DOMINANCE and RECESSIVENESS

If one gene of a pair can block the action of its partner, or allele, while still producing its own effect, that gene is said to be dominant over its allele. Its allele, on the other hand, is said to be recessive. In the case of heterozygous genes for eye color, the brown eye gene is dominant over the recessive blue eye gene, and the offspring therefore will have brown eyes. Much less common is the occurrence of gene pairs in which neither gene is completely dominant over the other. This, known as IN-COMPLETE or PARTIAL DOMINANCE, results in a blending of the

74

MENDELIAN EXPECTATION CHART

Pictured are the six possible ways in which a pair of genes can unite. The white boxes represent dominant genes; the black boxes represent recessives. Half of the genes of the sire will unite with half of the genes of the dam, and the expected results of such a mating are shown in the progeny combinations. Ratios apply to expectancy over large litters, except in lines 1, 2 and 6 where expectancy is realized in every litter (the exception due to mutation).

opposing influences. In cattle, if a homozygous (pure) red bull is mated with a homozygous (pure) white cow, the calf will be roan, a blending of red and white hairs in its coat, rather than either all red or all white.

During meiosis, or division of the reproductive (sperm and egg) cells, each pair of chromosomes splits, and one-half of each pair goes into one of the two new cells. Thus, in the case of eye color genes, one new reproductive cell will get the chromosome carrying the blue eye gene, while the other new reproductive cell will get the chromosome carrying the brown eye gene, and so on for each pair of chromosomes. If an organism has only one pair of chromosomes—called pair A, made up of chromosomes A_1 and A_2, and pair B, made up of chromosomes B_1 and B_2—each new reproductive cell will get one chromosome from each pair, and four different combinations are possible: A_1 and B_1; A_1 and B_2; A_2 and B_1; or A_2 and B_2. If the blue eye gene is on A_1, the brown eye gene on A_2, and the gene for curly hair on B_1, and the gene for straight hair on B_2, each of the above combinations will exert a different genetic effect on the offspring. This different grouping of chromosomes in the new reproductive cell as a result of meiotic cell division is known as *INDEPENDENT ASSORTMENT* and is one reason why variation occurs in the offspring. In the dog, with 39 pairs of chromosomes, the possibilites of variation through independent assortment are tremendous.

But variation does not end here. For example, if two dominant genes, such as the genes for brown eyes and dark hair, were on the same chromosome, all brown-eyed people would have dark hair. Yet in instances where such joined or *LINKED* genes do occur, the two characteristics do not always appear together in the same offspring. This is due to a process known as a *CROSS-OVER* or *RECOMBINATION*. Recombination is the mutual exchange of corresponding blocks of genes between the two chromosomes in a pair. That is, during cell division, the two chromosomes may exchange their tip sections or other corresponding segments. If the segments exchanged contain the eye color genes, the brown eye gene will be transferred from the chromosome carrying the dark hair gene to the chromosome carrying the light hair gene, and then brown eyes will occur with light hair, provided that the individual is homozygous for the recessive light hair gene.

Another important source of variation is *MUTATION*. In mutation, a gene becomes altered, such as by exposure to irradiation, and exerts a different effect than it did before. Most mutations are harmful to the organism, and some may result in death. Offspring carrying mutated genes and showing the effects of these mutations are known as *MUTANTS* or *SPORTS*. Mutation also means that instead of only two alleles for eye color, such as brown and blue, there may now be three or more (gray, black, etc.) creating a much larger source for possible variation in the offspring.

Further complications in the transmission and appearance of genetic traits are the phenomena known as *EPISTATIS* and *PLEIOTROPY*. Epistatis refers to a gene exerting influence on genes other than its own allele. In all-white red-eyed (albino) guinea pigs, for example, the gene controlling intensity of color is epistatic to any other color gene and prevents that gene from producing its effect. Thus, even if a gene for red spots were present in the cells of the guinea pig, the color intensity gene would prevent the red spots from appearing in the guinea pig's white coat. *Pleiotropy* refers to the fact that a single gene may control a number of characteristics. In the fruit fly, for example, the gene that controls eye color may also affect the structure of certain body parts and even the lifespan of the insect.

One special pair of chromosomes is known as the sex chromosomes. In man, dog, and other mammals, these chromosomes are of two types, designated as X and Y. Under normal conditions, a mammal carrying one X-type and one Y-type is a male. Females have two X chromosomes and can only contribute X chromosomes to the offspring, but the male can contribute either an X or a Y.

If the male's sperm carrying an X chromosome fertilizes the female's egg cell (X), the offspring (XX) will be a female; if a sperm carrying a Y chromosome fertilizes the egg (X), the offspring (XY) will be male. It is the male, therefore, that determines the sex of the offspring in mammals.

Traits controlled by genes present on the sex chromosome, and which appear in only one sex, are said to be *SEX LINKED*. If, for example, a rare recessive gene occurs on the X chromosome, it cannot exert its effect in the female because the dominant allele on the other X chromosomes will counteract it. In the male, however, there is no second X chromosome, and if the Y chromosome cannot offer any countereffect, the recessive character will appear. There are also *SEX-LIMITED* characteristics: these appear primarily or solely in one sex, but the genes for these traits are not carried on the sex chromosomes. Sex-limited traits appear when genes on other chromosomes exert their effect in the proper hormonal (male or female) environment. Sex-linked and sex-limited transmission is how a trait may skip a generation, by being passed from grandfather to grandson through a mother in which the trait, though present, does not show.

In dealing with the simplest form of heredity—one gene effecting one character—there is an expected ratio of the offspring displaying the character to those who do not display it, depending upon the genetic makeup of the parents. If a parent is homozygous for a character, such as blue eyes, it makes no difference which half of the chromosome pair enters the new reproductive cell, because each chromosome carries the gene for blue eyes. If a parent is heterozygous, however, one reproductive cell will receive the brown eye gene while the other will receive the blue eye gene. If both parents are homozygous for blue eyes, all the offspring will receive two blue eye genes, and all will have blue eyes. If a parent is homozygous for blue eyes, and the other parent is homozygous for brown eyes, all the offspring will be heterozygous, receiving one brown eye and one blue eye gene, and because brown is dominant, all will have brown eyes. If both parents are heterozygous, both the blue eye gene and the brown eye gene from one parent have an equal likelihood of ending up with either the blue eye or the brown eye gene from the other parent. This results in a ratio of two heterozygous offspring to the one homozygous for brown eyes and one homozygous for blue eyes, giving a total genetic, or genotypic, ratio of 2:1:1 or, as it is more commonly arranged, 1:2:1. As the two heterozygous as well as the homozygous brown eye offspring will have brown eyes, the ratio of brown eyes to blue eyes (or phenotypic ratio) will be 3:1.

If one parent is heterozygous and the other parent is homozygous for the recessive gene for blue eyes, but the other half of the offspring will be heterozygous and have brown eyes. (Here both the genotypic and phenotypic ratio is 1:1.)

If the homozygous parent, however, has the dominant gene (brown eyes), half of the offspring will be heterozygous and half will be homozygous, as before, but all will have brown eyes. By repeated determinations of these ratios in the offspring, geneticists are able to analyze the genetic makeup of the parents.

Before leaving heredity, it might be well to explain the difference between inbreeding, outcrossing, line breeding, and similar terms. Basically, there are only inbreeding and outbreeding. Inbreeding, however, according to its intensity, is usually divided into interbreeding proper and line breeding. Inbreeding proper is considered to be the mating of very closely related individuals, generally within the immediate family, but this is sometimes extended to include matings to first cousins and grandparents. Line breeding is the mating of more distantly related animals, that is, animals not immediately related to each other but having a common ancestor, such as the same grandsire or great-grandsire. Outbreeding is divided into outcrossing, which is the mating of dogs from different families within the same breed, and cross-breeding, which is mating purebred dogs from different breeds.

From the foregoing discussion of genetics, it should be realized that the theory of telegony, which states that the sire of one litter can influence future litters sired by other studs, is simply not true; it is possible, however, if several males mate with a female during a single estrus cycle, that the various puppies in the litter may have different sires (but not two sires for any one puppy). It should also be realized that blood does not really enter into the transmission of inheritance, although people commonly speak of "bloodlines," "pure-blooded," etc.

7. CARE OF THE MOTHER AND THE NEW FAMILY

PRENATAL CARE OF THE FEMALE

You can expect the puppies nine weeks from the day of breeding, although 58 days is as common as 63. During this time the female should receive normal care and exercise. If she is overweight, don't increase her food at first; excess weight at whelping time is not good. If she is on the thin side, build her up, giving her a morning meal of cereal and egg yolk. Consult your veterinarian as to increasing her vitamins and mineral supplement. During the last weeks the puppies grow enormously, and the mother will have little room for food and less appetite. Divide her meals into smaller portions and feed her more often. If she loses her appetite, tempt her with meat, liver, chicken, etc.

As she grows heavier, eliminate violent exercise and jumping. Do not eliminate exercise entirely, as walking is beneficial to the female in whelp, and mild exercise will maintain her muscle tone in preparation for the birth. Weigh your female after breeding and keep a record of her weight each week thereafter. Groom your bitch daily—some females have a slight discharge during gestation, more prevalent during the last two weeks, so wash the vulva with warm water daily. Usually, by the end of the fifth week you can notice a broadening across her loins, and her breasts become firmer. By the end of the sixth week your veterinarian can tell you whether or not she is pregnant.

PREPARATION OF WHELPING QUARTERS

Prepare a whelping box a few days before the puppies are due, and allow the mother to sleep there overnight or to spend some time in it during the day to become accustomed to it. Then she is less likely to try to have her pups under the front porch or in the middle of your bed. The box should have a wooden floor. Sides about a foot high will keep the puppies in but enable the mother to get out after she has fed them. If the weather is cold, the box should be raised about an inch off the floor.

You should place a guard rail in the whelping box to prevent the mother from rolling over onto the pups and smothering them. This guard is a strip of wood which will project out and above the floor of the box, keeping the bitch from pressing up against the sides of the box.

GUARD RAIL

SIDE BOARDS - ADDED LATER

STEP

ONE SIDE HINGED
FOR EASY CLEANING

WHELPING BOX

Layers of newspaper spread over the whole area will make excellent bedding and be absorbent enough to keep the surface warm and dry. They should be removed daily and replaced with another thick layer. An old quilt or washable blanket makes better footing for the nursing puppies than slippery newspaper during the first week, and is softer for the mother. The quilt should be secured firmly.

SUPPLIES TO HAVE ON HAND

As soon as you have the whelping box prepared, set up the nursery by collecting the various supplies you will need when the puppies arrive. You should have the following items on hand: a box lined with towels for the puppies, a heating pad or hot water bottle to keep the puppy box warm, a pile of clean terrycloth towels or washcloths to remove membranes and to dry puppies, a stack of folded newspapers, a roll of paper towels, vaseline, rubber gloves, soap, iodine, muzzle, cotton balls, a small pair of blunt scissors to cut umbilical cords (place scissors into an open bottle of alcohol so they keep freshly sterilized), a rectal thermometer, white thread, a flashlight in case the electricity goes off, a waste container, and a scale for weighing each puppy at birth.

It is necessary that the whelping room be warm and free from drafts, because puppies are delivered wet from the mother. Keep a little notebook and pencil handy so you can record the duration of the first labor and the time between the arrival of each puppy. If there is trouble in whelping, this is the information that the veterinarian will want. Keep his telephone number handy in case you have to call him in an emergency, and warn him to be prepared for an emergency, should you need him.

WHELPING

Be prepared for the actual whelping several days in advance. Usually the female will tear up papers, try to dig nests, refuse food, and generally act restless and nervous. These may be false alarms; the real test is her temperature, which will drop to below 100ºF about twelve hours before whelping. Take her temperature rectally at a set time each day, starting about a week before she is due to whelp. After her temperature goes down, keep her constantly with you or put her in the whelping box and stay in the room with her. She will seem anxious and look to you for reassurance. During the birth, if neccesary, be prepared to remove the membranes covering the puppy's head if the mother fails to do this, for the puppy could smother otherwise.

The mother should start licking the puppy as soon as it is out of the sac, thus drying and stimulating it, but if she does not perform this task you can do it with a rough towel, instead. The afterbirth should follow the birth of each puppy, attached to the puppy by the umbilical cord. Watch to make sure that each is expelled, for retaining this material can cause infection. The mother probably will eat the afterbirth after biting the cord. One or two will not hurt her; they stimulate milk supply as well as labor for remaining puppies. Too many, however, can make her lose her appetite for the food she needs to feed her puppies and regain her strength, so remove the rest of them along with the soiled newspaper, and keep the box dry and clean to relieve her anxiety.

If a puppy does not start breathing, wrap him in a towel, hold him upside down with his head toward the ground, and shake him vigorously. If he still does not breathe, rub his ribs briskly; if this also fails, administer artificial respiration by compressing his ribs about twenty times per minute.

If the mother does not bite the cord, or bites it too close to the body, you should take over the job to prevent an umbilical hernia. Cut the cord a short distance from the body with your blunt scissors. Put a drop of iodine on the end of the cord; it will dry up and fall off in a few days.

The puppies should follow each other at regular intervals, but deliveries can be as short as five minutes or as long as two hours apart. A puppy may be presented backwards; if the mother does not seem to be in trouble, *do not interfere.* But if enough of the puppy is outside the birth canal, use a rough towel and help her by pulling gently on the puppy.

Pull only when she pushes. A rear-first, or breech birth can cause a puppy to strangle on its own umbilical cord, so don't let the mother struggle too long. Breech birth is quite common.

When you think all the puppies have been whelped, have your veterinarian examine the mother to determine if all the afterbirths have been expelled. He will probably give her an injection to be certain that the uterus is clean, a shot of calcium for prevention of eclampsia, and possibly an injection of penicillin to prevent infection.

CAESAREAN SECTION

Sometimes a Caesarean section is necessary, although very rarely. The operation of removing the pups by cutting into the abdomen and uterus of the bitch is generally safe; however, if the emergency Caesarean section follows a prolonged, exhausting and fruitless labor, the danger to the bitch is substantially increased.

Reasons for resorting to a Caesarean section include: 1. dystocia due to an abnormally large pup, 2. one presenting in such a way that it cannot get out, is blocking the passage and birth of its littermates or is threatening the life of its dam, 3. an abnormal pelvis in the bitch which does not allow passage of the pups (such as a previous pelvic fracture), 4. inertia, 5. long and arduous labor which exhausts the bitch to the point where weakness causes the uterine and abdominal contractions to stop.

Your bitch can be operated on without losing consciousness if your veterinarian selects to operate with a hypnotic and local anesthesia. The local anesthesia is injected, the incision made, and the pups taken from the semi-conscious bitch.

Gas anesthesia is the safest type of general anesthetic for delivering pups; if barbiturate anesthetics are used intravenously, the puppies may be quite effected by these drugs as they pass through the placental barrier.

Regardless of which method is used for the Caesarean section, the patient should be kept in a warm, clean bed after surgery until she recovers from the anesthesia. The pups should not be placed with the dam until she is once again alert. If the pups are also depressed from the anesthetic, artificial respiration may be required. It is imperative that the pups be kept dry and warm following the delivery.

Offer the puppies to their mother one at a time. After she licks a pup, help it to get settled on a teat and observe them carefully. Rarely, the bitch may not accept her puppies, but this may only be a temporary situation. Watch the mother when she goes out to do her duties; her sutures (stitches) should not be subjected to any undue strain. A binder may interfere with emptying several breasts, but aside from this she will behave in a normal manner. The stitches will be removed in about two weeks and she will be as good as new.

In the cases of both normal and Caesarean delivery the female's temperature should be checked twice daily for one week after delivery. A temperature of over 102°F should be reported to your veterinarian and his directions followed to the letter.

ECLAMPSIA

Eclampsia, or "milk fever," is caused by a lowered calcium content of the blood, due to the bitch's depleting her body's calcium reserves for the production of milk. It is a word that has been fearsome in the dog-breeding world for many years. If it occurs after whelping, the puppies and the mother are in severe danger. Help must be given immediately. The female stiffens her legs, has pale gums, and is likely to have minor convulsions. Puppies must be taken from her and calcium and dextrose administered to her intravenously. However, this is a rare thing and the symptoms so obvious, that assuredly the owner's first thought is that something is wrong and that the veterinarian is needed at once. With proper nutrition during gestation and lactation, a lack of calcium is not to be expected. The best preventive medicine is to see that the female is parasite free, in good condition, and properly cared for from the day she is mated.

HOW TO TAKE CARE OF A LARGE LITTER

The size of a litter varies greatly. If your bitch has a large litter she may have trouble feeding all of the puppies. You can help her by preparing an extra puppy box. Leave half the litter with the mother and the other half in a warm place, changing their places at two-hour intervals at first. Later you may change them less frequently, leaving them all together except during the day. Try supplementary feeding, too, as soon as their eyes are open, since at about two weeks they will lap from a dish.

RAISING THE PUPPIES

Hold each puppy to a breast as soon as he is dry, for a good meal without competition. Then he may join his littermates in the basket, out of his mother's way, while she is whelping. Keep a supply of evaporated milk on hand for emergencies, or later weaning. A formula of evaporated milk, corn syrup and a little water with egg yolk should be warmed and fed in a doll or baby bottle if necessary. A supplementary feeding often helps weak pups over the hump. Keep track of birth weights and take weekly readings so you will have an accurate record of the pups' growth and health.

This compartmentalized incubator demonstrates one method of caring for orphaned puppies. Orphaned pups need to be kept warm by artificial means since they do not have their mother to cuddle next to.

After the puppies have arrived, take the mother outside for a walk and drink, and then leave her to take care of them. She will probably not want to stay away more than a minute or two for the first few weeks. Be sure to keep water available at all times, and feed her milk or broth frequently, as she needs liquids to produce milk. To encourage her to eat, offer her the foods she likes best, until she asks to be fed without your tempting her. She will soon develop a ravenous appetite and should have at least two large meals a day, with dry food available in addition.

Prepare a warm place to put the puppies after they are born to keep them dry and help them to a good start in life. Cover an electric heating pad or hot-water bottle with flannel and put it in the bottom of a cardboard box. Set the box near the mother so that she can see her puppies. She will usually allow you to help, but don't take the puppies out of sight, and let her handle things if your interference seems to make her nervous.

Be sure that all of the puppies are getting enough to eat. If the mother sits or stands, instead of lying still to nurse, the probable cause is scratching from the puppies's nails. You can remedy this by clipping them, as you do hers. Manicure scissors will do for these tiny claws.

The puppies should normally be completely weaned at six weeks, although you start to feed them at three weeks. They will find it easier to lap semi-solid food. At four weeks they will eat four meals a day, and soon do without their mother entirely. Start them on mixed dog food, or leave it with them in a dish for self-feeding. Don't leave water with them all the time; at this age everything is to play with and they will use it as a wading pool. They can drink all they need if it is offered several times a day, after meals.

As the puppies grow up the mother will go into the pen only to nurse them, first sitting up and then standing. To dry her up completely, keep the mother away for longer periods, and then completely. The little milk left will be reabsorbed.

AIRING THE PUPPIES

The puppies may be put outside, unless it is too cold, as soon as their eyes are open. They will benefit from the sunlight and the vitamin D it provides. A rubber mat or newspapers underneath will protect them from cold or damp.

WORMING

You can expect a litter of pups to need at least one worming before they are ready to go to new homes, so take a stool sample to your veterinarian at about six weeks of age. Also, the litter should receive their first temporary shots, which are usually distemper-hepatitis-leptospirosis globulin. Today many kennels are advised by veterinarians to administer these preventative shots even earlier than six weeks, and in special cases they may begin right after birth. The puppy derives immunity from his mother's milk during the first twenty-four hours of his life; this immunity lasts for a varying length of time. Some mothers do not offer any immunity to their young at all. Therefore, in a kennel where the exposure rate is high, and many dogs come and go to shows, and disease may easily be brought to the premises, prophylactic treatment must start early. In the average home, where there is one female and one litter, six weeks is the proper time to start this treatment, and it must be repeated every one to two weeks until the puppies are old enough to have their permanent shots.

PUPPY SOCIALIZATION

Animal psychologists, research scientists and people who train dogs to work closely with people, such as trainers of seeing-eye dogs, have found that the first few weeks of a puppy's life is a critical time. The treatment a puppy receives during this stage determines whether he will become a mentally stable, trustworthy dog that likes people and is able to fit into their particular lifestyle. In general, the dog that is to be a reliable show dog or loving pet must be cuddled often, and experience pleasurable associations with people from a very early age. It is the duty of every creditable breeder to be willing to commit the amount of time necessary to socialize his puppies before he decides to breed his bitch. The behavior of his puppies, whether they are show prospects or pets, reflects on the breed and on his kennel name, two very good reasons for giving the puppies the kind of exposure to human companionship that will turn them into desirable adult dogs. This is not to deny heredity, but to stress the importance of human association in the early weeks of a puppy's life.

Some experts feel that the first three weeks of a puppy's life are completely taken up with nursing, sleeping and keeping warm snuggling with his littermates and dam, and that people-geared socialization should begin after these first three weeks. Others feel that it should begin right away, but that the form varies with the age. During the first weeks while the puppy is still gaining strength and weight and until his eyes are open, socialization should consist of simply holding the tiny pup, stroking its back and tummy for a few minutes and then putting it back with its mother. This should take place with each puppy, every day. As the puppy grows older, the time can be lengthened.

When the puppies are old enough to start eating solid foods, you can reinforce the pleasure contact by feeding them by hand. Basic training and developing receptivity to further training when they are older takes place at this point, so when you call them to you for the hand-held food, always use the same catch phrase. When the puppies are about a month old it's time to reinforce their sense of self-sufficiency and ease in new surroundings. This will also ease the transition to a new home. Remove the pups from their whelping box, which until now has circumscribed nearly their entire world, and take them to a different scene. The pup with the most adaptable nature is the one who will immediately move about and begin to explore this new setting. Puppies that are frightened and do not relax after a short time in this new environment should be put back with their mates until next time.

When they are six weeks old, puppies can be further disposed to training by putting a collar on them so they will get used to the feeling of it. Then put on the leash, not to take them for a walk, but just to let them run around in it so they get used to the idea. Later, more serious training can take place by the new owner with the puppy that is taking his place as a temperamentally sound, self-assured, friendly youngster in the world of his human companions.

8. GENERAL HEALTH CARE

WATCHING YOUR PUPPY'S HEALTH

First, don't be frightened by the number of diseases a dog can contract. The majority of dogs never get any of them. Don't become a dog-hypochondriac. All dogs have days when they feel lazy and want to lie around doing nothing. For the few diseases that you might be concerned about, remember that your veterinarian is your dog's best friend. When you first get your puppy, select a veterinarian whom you have faith in. He will get to know your dog and will be glad to have you consult him for advice. A dog needs little medical care, but that little is essential to his good health and well-being. He needs:

1. Proper diet at regular hours
2. Clean, roomy housing
3. Daily exercise
4. Companionship and love
5. Frequent grooming
6. Regular check-ups by your veterinarian

THE USEFUL THERMOMETER

Almost every serious ailment shows itself by an increase in the dog's body temperature. If your dog acts lifeless, looks dull-eyed, and gives the impression of illness, check his temperature by using a rectal thermometer. A stubby end rectal thermometer of either plastic or glass is best suited for this procedure. Although uncommon, there is always the hazard of possible breakage should he become excited during insertion. However, he is easily calmed if you soothe him when the routine is taking place. Hold the dog securely, and insert the thermometer, which you have lubricated with vaseline, and take a reading. The average normal temperature for your dog will be 101.5 °F. Excitement may raise the temperature slightly, but any rise of more than a few points is cause for alarm, and your vet should be consulted.

EMERGENCY FIRST AID

In general, a dog will heal his wounds by licking them. If he swallows anything harmful, chances are that he will throw it up. But it will probably make you feel better to help him if he is hurt, so treat his wounds as you would your own. Wash out the dirt and apply an antiseptic.

If you fear that your dog has swallowed poison, get him to the veterinarian's *at once*. In the meantime, try and locate the source of poisoning; if he has swallowed, for example, a cleaning fluid kept in your house, check the bottle label to see if inducing the dog to vomit is necessary. In some cases, inducing the dog to vomit can be very harmful, depending upon the type of poison swallowed. Amateur diagnosis is very dangerous, when you consider that time is so extremely important.

Accidents

Accidents, unfortunately, will happen so it is best to be prepared. If your dog gets hit by a car, keep him absolutely quiet, move him as little as possible and get veterinary treatment as soon as possible. It is unwise to give any stimulants such as brandy or other alcoholic liquids where there is visible external hemorrhage or the possibility of internal hemorrhaging. If your dog has cut his foot or leg badly, on glass or otherwise, bandage the wound as tightly as possible to stop the bleeding. A wad of cotton may serve as a pressure bandage, which will ordinarily stop the flow of blood. Gauze wrapped around the cotton will hold it in place. Usually, applying such pressure to a wound will sufficiently stop the blood flow; however, for severe bleeding, such as when an artery is cut, a tourniquet may be necessary. Apply a tourniquet between the injury and the heart if the bleeding is severe. To tighten the tourniquet, push a pencil through the bandage and twist it. Take your dog to a veterinarian immediately since a tourniquet should not be left in place any longer than fifteen minutes.

Blood coming from an artery is bright red in color and will spurt in unison with the heart beat. From a vein, it is dark red and continuous in flow.

Burns and Scalds

Any dog kept in the home runs the risk of being burned or scalded at one time or another. If your pet sustains a serious burn, call the vet immediately as shock quickly follows such a burn. The dog should be kept warm and quiet, wrapped in a blanket. If he still shows signs of being chilled, use a hot water bottle. Clean the burn gently, removing any foreign matter such as bits of lint, hair, grass or dirt. Act as quickly as possible. Prevent exposure to air by applying olive oil or another similar substance and cover with gauze, cotton and a loose bandage. To prevent the dog from interfering with the dressing, muzzle him and have someone stay with him until veterinary treatment is at hand.

If the burn or scald is a minor one clip hair away from the affected area and apply a paste of bicarbonate of soda and water. Apply it thickly to the burned area and try to keep the dog from licking it off.

Often the only way to adequately determine the best treatment for your dog is through microscopic analysis of a blood smear or tissue scraping so the veterinarian can diagnose the ailment exactly.

Snake Bite

If your dog is bitten by a poisonous snake, open up the wound with any available instrument that is sharp and clean. Squeeze the wound to cause a fair amount of blood to flow. This will wash the poison from the wound as much as possible. The dog should be taken to the veterinarian immediately so antitoxins can be administered. If the bite has been sustained on the leg, it is advisable to apply a tourniquet if at all possible to keep the poison from flowing further. Under no circumstances should snake bite from a poisonous snake, or its treatment, be taken lightly.

Stings

Many dogs enjoy trying to catch wasps and bees. When these insects are prevalent it is difficult to stop your pet from snapping at them. A sting frequently follows a successful catch and it often occurs inside the mouth, which can be very serious. The best remedy is to get him to a veterinarian as soon as possible, but there are some precautionary measures to follow in the meantime. If the dog has been lucky enough to only be caught on the outside of the face, try to extricate the stinger, then swab the point of entry with a solution of bicarbonate of soda. In the case of a wasp sting, use vinegar or some other acidic food stuff. A useful remedy for wasp stings is to rub the part with moistened tobacco, i.e., an unsmoked cigarette end that has been moistened.

IMPORTANCE OF INOCULATIONS

With the proper series of inoculations, your dog will be almost completely protected against disease. However, it occasionally happens that the shot does not take, and sometimes a different form of the virus appears against which your dog may not be protected.

Distemper

Probably the most virulent of all dog diseases is distemper. Young dogs are most susceptible to it, although it may affect dogs of all ages. The dog will lose his appetite, seem depressed, chilled, and run a fever. Often he will have a watery discharge from his eyes and nose. Unless treated promptly, the disease goes into advanced stages with infections of the lungs, intestines, and nervous system, and dogs that recover may be left with some impairment such as paralysis, convulsions, a twitch, or some other defect, usually spastic in nature. The best protection against this is very early inoculation with a series of permanent shots and a booster shot each year thereafter.

Hepatitis

Veterinarians report an increase in the spread of this viral disease in recent years, usually with younger dogs as the victims. The initial symptoms—drowsiness, vomiting, great thirst, loss of appetite, and a high temperature—closely resemble those of distemper. These symptoms are often accompanied by swellings of the head, neck, and abdomen. The disease strikes quickly; death may occur in just a few hours. Protection is afforded by injection with a vaccine recently developed.

Leptospirosis

This disease is carried by bacteria that live in stagnant or slow-moving water. It is carried by rats and dogs; infection is begun by the dog's licking substances contaminated by the urine or feces of infected animals. The symptoms are diarrhea and a yellowish-brownish discoloration of the jaws, tongue, and teeth, caused by an inflammation of the kidneys.

This disease can be cured if caught in time, but it is best to ward it off with a vaccine which your veterinarian can administer along with the distemper shots.

Rabies

This is an acute disease of the dog's central nervous system. It is spread by infectious saliva transmitted by the bite of an infected animal. Rabies is generally manifested in one of two classes of symptoms. The first is "furious rabies," in which the dog shows a period of melancholy or depression, then irritation, and finally paralysis. The first period lasts from a few hours to several days. During this time the dog is cross and will change his position often. He loses his appetite for food and begins to lick, bite and swallow foreign objects. During the irritative phase the dog is spasmodically wild and has impulses to run away. He acts in a fearless manner and runs at and bites everything in sight. If he is caged or confined he will fight at the bars, often breaking teeth or fracturing his jaw. His bark becomes a peculiar howl. In the final, or paralytic stage, the animal's lower jaw becomes paralyzed and hangs down; he walks with a stagger and saliva drips from his mouth. Within four to eight days after the onset of paralysis, the dog dies.

The second class of symptoms is referred to as "dumb rabies" and is characterized by the dog's walking in a bearlike manner, head down. The lower jaw is paralyzed and the dog is unable to bite. Outwardly, it may seem as though he had a bone caught in his throat.

Even if your pet should be bitten by a rabid dog or other animal, he probably can be saved if you get him to the veterinarian in time for a series of injections. However, after the symptoms have appeared no cure is possible. But remember that an annual rabies inoculation is almost certain protection against rabies. If you suspect that your dog has rabies, notify your local Health Department. A rabid dog is a danger to all who come near him.

HIP DYSPLASIA

This often crippling condition is more prevalent in large breeds than in small, but has occurred in almost every breed. The cause is not absolutely known though it is believed to be hereditary and as yet there is no known cure. The condition exists in varying degrees of severity. In general, hip dysplasia can be described as a poor fit between the two bones of the hip joint—the femur and the acetabulum—and is caused by a malformation of one or the other. Either the head of the femur is flattened causing it to slip out of the socket, or a shallowness of the acetabulum causes the femur to slip out. HD is usually graded according to severity and

Severely dysplastic hips, such as those pictured here, are incurable and hereditary. It is generally agreed that newborn puppies do not phenotypically exhibit the hip dysplasia trait and they begin life with properly fitted hips. The first signs of hip dysplasia become noticeable as unsteady movement in puppies at several months of age. Sometimes the gait of the puppy appears normal, but he tires very easily. The length of the stride is usually limited. The condition worsens with age, as the rim of the hip socket slowly wears down until there is no longer a proper fit between the femoral head of the hip bone and the hip socket. Since a predisposition for the disease is passed from parent to offspring, it is imperative that no dog exhibiting signs of hip dysplasia be used for breeding.

poorness of fit between the ball and socket, with the lowest grades being the best fit and the higher end of the scale denoting the worst cases.

HD causes stiffness in the hindlegs, considerable pain in the more severe cases and difficulty of movement. It generally manifests itself in puppyhood and can be noticed by the time the young dog is two months old. Severity can usually be determined by the age of six months. If HD is suspected, the dog should be x-rayed, and if afflicted it should not be used for breeding. Cases vary greatly, but severe pain may be more or less continuous in advanced cases. When this is true euthanasia is occasionally recommended, though medication is available to control the pain and allow the dog to move with more ease. Rigorous exercise is not recommended since it only increases the rate at which the bone surfaces wear away.

COUGHS, COLDS, BRONCHITIS, PNEUMONIA

Respiratory diseases may affect the dog because he is forced to live under man-made conditions rather than in his natural environment. Being subjected to cold or a draft after a bath, sleeping near an air conditioner or in the path of a fan or near a radiator can cause respiratory ailments. The symptoms are similar to those in humans. The germs of these diseases, however, are different and do not affect both dogs and humans, so they cannot be infected by each other. Treatment is much the same as for a child with the same type of illness. Keep the dog warm, quiet, and well fed. Your veterinarian has antibiotics and other remedies to help the dog recover.

DIABETES MELLITUS (Sugar Diabetes)

This is a disease wherein the sugar balance of the body is disturbed because of insufficient production of the hormone insulin. The pancreas secretes insulin which regulates carbohydrate/sugar usage. When the insulin-producing cells are damaged, the condition arises. It is marked by an increase in the blood sugar level and an excessive amount of sugar is excreted in the urine.

Symptoms of the condition are great thirst, increased urination and loss of weight while the appetite and food consumption increases. The signs vary in severity. If overlooked, emaciation and collapse rapidly occur. The dog can go into a diabetic coma and die.

Treatment is the same as for human diabetes, utilizing dietary regulation and insulin injections if necessary. The diet should be one of very low fat, with a low percentage of carbohydrate and a higher pecentage of protein. The insulin dose must be adjusted as indicated by urine tests which your veterinarian can teach you to administer at home. The test makes use of chemically treated sticks, pale yellow in color, which turn to various shades of green when dipped in urine. The darker the shade, the more serious the condition.

INTERNAL PARASITES

There are four common internal parasites that may infect your dog. These are roundworms, hookworms, whipworms, and tapeworms. The first three can be diagnosed by laboratory examination; the presence of tapeworms is determined by seeing segments in the stool or attached to the hair around the tail. Do not under any circumstances attempt to worm your dog without the advice of your veterinarian. After first determining what type of worm or worms are present, he will advise you of the best method of treatment.

A dog or puppy in good physical condition is less susceptible to worm infestation than a weak dog. Proper sanitation and a nutritious diet help in preventing worms. One of the best preventative measures is to always have clean, dry bedding for your dog. This will diminish the possibility of reinfection due to flea or tick bites.

Heartworms

Heartworm infestation in dogs is passed by mosquitoes and can be a life threatening problem. Dogs with the disease tire easily, have difficulty breathing, cough and may lose weight despite a hearty appetite. If caught in the early stages, the disease can be effectively treated; however, the administration of daily preventative medicine throughout the spring, summer and fall months is strongly advised. Your veterinarian must first take

Pictured is the heart of a dog showing a heavy infestation of heartworms. Mosquitoes carry the offspring of the adult worms which are implanted into a dog's bloodstream when the dog is bitten. The worm offspring travel to the heart where they do their damage as they develop into adult worms. U.S.D.A.

94

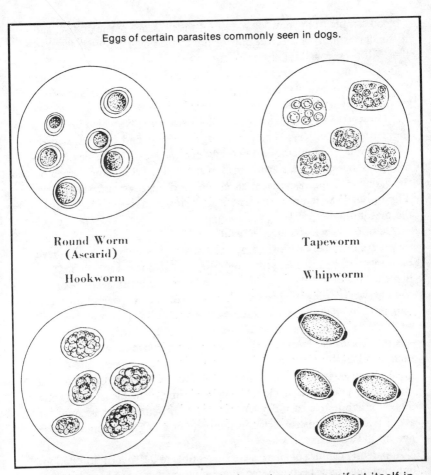

Eggs of certain parasites commonly seen in dogs.

Round Worm
(Ascarid)

Tapeworm

Hookworm

Whipworm

The presence of worms in your dog's system can manifest itself in outward signs such as a general deterioration, loss of weight, dulling of coat, diarrhea and vomiting. *Roundworm* larvae penetrate the intestinal lining, where they enter the bloodstream and are carried to the lungs. This worm affects mostly puppies, in whom it can cause lung damage and intestinal blockage. There are many species of *tapeworm* that can infest your dog. The important factor in breaking the life cycle of the tapeworm is the elimination of the parasitic host on which the worm thrives. Fleas are perhaps the most common host, so ridding your dog of them is a step toward eliminating the possibility of tapeworm infection. If present in massive quantities, *hookworms*, which remove blood from the dog, may cause circulatory collapse and ultimate death. *Whipworms* may cause weight loss, vomiting, diarrhea and secondary anemia in an affected dog.

a blood sample from your dog to test for the presence of the disease, and if the dog is heartworm-free, pills or liquid medicine can be prescribed that will protect against any infestation.

It was formerly believed that heartworms occured only in warmer climates, but it is now known that they may occur anywhere that they can be carried by any of several species of mosquitoes.

Adult worms are found in the right side of the heart, the vena cavae and the pulmonary artery. There the eggs develop and are released as microfilariae. The microfilariae circulate in the blood of the dog until a mosquito ingests them, starting the larval growth cycle. Being carried by the various mosquito species induces the third-stage larval development. The third-stage larvae are re-deposited during a subsequent feeding by the mosquito and proceed to grow.

Microfilariae remain inactive while in the blood of the dog in which they were originally deposited by the female. It is only after they have been ingested by a subsequent mosquito and redeposited in another host that they begin to develop. These larvae lodge in subcutaneous tissue or muscle where they stay about three months; at between three and four months they migrate to the heart. Three to four months later the adult worm begins producing microfilariae.

Adult worms are creamy white in color. The female grows to 11 or 12 inches in length, the male, to six or seven inches. The sexes are distinquished by length since both are about the diameter of the lead in a mechanical pencil. Each mature female worm is capable of producing 30,000 microfilariae each day. A hundred adult females can account for about two billion microfilariae in the body of a dog since microfilariae live up to two years.

Apparently canines of all ages are susceptible to heartworm infestation, but they must have been exposed to mosquitoes in order to have acquired the third-stage infective larvae. Heartworm infection increases markedly as the dog matures. If left undetected, it will erode the heart.

A microscopic search for microfilariae is necessary to prove that adult worms are present. Because of the large number and size of the worms, treatment must be careful and slow to minimize damage to the circulatory system.

SKIN AILMENTS

Any persistent scratching may indicate an irritation. Whenever you groom your dog, look for the reddish spots that may indicate eczema, mange, or fungal infection. Rather than treating your dog yourself, take him to the veterinarian, as some of the conditions may be difficult to eradicate and can cause permanent damage to his coat.

Two of the most common external parasites are the tick (left) and the flea (right). Along with the general discomfort and irritation that they bring to your dog, these parasites can infest him with worms and disease. The flea is a carrier of tapeworm, and may act as an intermediate host for heartworm. The tick can cause dermatitis and anemia in your dog, and may also be a carrier of Rocky Mountain spotted fever and canine babesiasis, a blood infection.

External Parasites

The dog that is groomed regularly and provided with clean sleeping quarters should not be troubled by fleas, ticks, or lice. If the dog should become infested with any of these parasites, he should be treated with medicated dip bath or the new oral medications that are presently available.

Mange

There are two types of mange, sarcoptic and follicular, both of which are caused by a parasite. The former is by far the more common, and results in an intense irritation, causing violent scratching. Close examination will reveal small red spots which become filled with pus. This is a highly contagious condition, and any dog showing signs of the disease should be isolated. Consult your veterinarian for the proper treatment procedures. Follicular mange is very much harder to cure, but fortunately, it is much rarer and less contagious. This disease will manifest itself as bare patches appearing on the skin, which becomes thickened and leathery. A complete cure from this condition is only rarely effected.

Eczema

This disease occurs most often in the summer months and affects the dog down the back, especially just above the root of the tail. It should not be confused with mange, as it is not caused by a parasite. One of the principle causes of eczema is improper nutrition, which makes the dog susceptible to disease. Hot, humid weather predisposes the growth of bacteria, which can invade a susceptible dog and thereby cause skin irritations and lesions. It is imperative that the dog gets relief from the itching that is symptomatic of the disease as this self-mutilation by scratching will only help to spread the inflammation. Antibiotics may be necessary if a bacterial infection is, indeed, present. The dog must be thoroughly ridded of fleas to avoid any recurrance of the scratching that can spread the disease.

Moist eczema, commonly referred to as "hot spots," is a rapidly appearing skin disease that produces a moist infection. Spots appear very suddenly and may spread rapidly in a few hours, infecting several parts of the body. These lesions are generally bacterially infected and are extremely itchy, which will cause the dog to scratch frantically and further damage the afflicted areas. Vomiting, fever and an enlargement of the lymph nodes may occur. The infected areas must be clipped to the skin and thoroughly cleaned. Your veterinarian will prescribe an anti-inflammatory drug and antibiotics, as well as a soothing emollient to relieve itching.

EYES, EARS, TEETH AND NAILS

If your dog is to remain in good health, you must be aware of the need for periodic "examinations" in which you routinely inspect him for unusual signs of irritation or infection. In most cases, the tell-tale warning signals are any unusual swelling, discharge or redness that may appear, especially after an injury.

The eyes, because of their sensitivity, are prone to injury and infection. Dogs that spend a great deal of time outdoors in heavily wooded areas may return from an exercise excursion with watery eyes, the result of brambles and high weeds scratching them. The eyes may also be irritated by dirt and other foreign matter.

Should your dog's eyes appear red and watery, a mild solution can be mixed at home for a soothing washing. Your veterinarian will be able to tell you what percentage of boric acid, salt, or other medicinal compound to mix with water.

You must monitor your dog's eyes after such a solution is administered; if the irritation persists, or if there is a significant discharge, immediate veterinary attention is warranted.

Your dog's ears, like his eyes, are extremely sensitive and can also be prone to infection, should wax and/or dirt be allowed to build up. Ear irritants may be present in the form of mites, soap or water, or foreign par-

The Elizabethan collar is designed to keep your dog from scratching the area about his head and ears when a wound or sutures there advise against scratching. While they can be purchased ready-made, they can also be easily made at home from a piece of cardboard box. Be sure the hole is large enough so that it does not constrict the dog's breathing or swallowing.

ticles which the dog has come into contact with while romping through a wooded area. If your dog's ears are bothering him, you will know it—he will scratch and paw them, shake his head, and the ears will show a foul-smelling dark secretion. This pasty secretion usually signals the onset of *otorrhea*, or ear canker, and at this stage proper veterinary care is essential if the dog's hearing is not to be permanently impaired. In the advanced stages of ear canker, tissue builds up within the ear, and the ear canal becomes blocked off, thus eliminating the hearing abilities of that ear.

If this is to be prevented, you should wash your dog's ears as they require it, with a very dilute solution of hydrogen peroxide and water, or an antibacterial ointment, as your vet suggests. In any case, the ears, because of their delicacy, are to be washed gently, with a soft cloth or cotton.

The good health of your pet's teeth can be maintained by his regular use of a chew product such as Nylabone® or Nylaball®, which serves to clean the teeth of tartar accumulation and massage and stimulate the gums. With puppies, a chew product helps to relieve the discomfort of the teething stage, and of course prevents the pup's chewing of your furniture and slippers!

A periodic inspection of your dog's mouth will alert you to any problem he might have that would require a trip to the veterinarian's office. Any signs of tooth or gum sensitivity, redness or swelling, signal the need for professional treatment. Also, it is best to have your pet's teeth scraped once or twice a year, at the time that he goes to the vet's for his general physical check-up. This simple procedure removes any excess tartar that

Badly decayed teeth can cause abscesses of mouth tissues and gums, and even bone deterioration in extreme cases. Pain caused by such a condition can discourage your dog from eating even though he is hungry, resulting in possible malnutrition or even starvation. Your vet should be consulted if any listlessness or change in eating habits is noticed.

Dog nail clippers are designed to trim nails quickly and easily with a minimum of scuffling between you and your dog. While other general purpose instruments can be used, there is a greater chance with these of cutting too far down on the nail and hitting the vein, resulting in a painful experience for your dog.

has accumulated on his teeth that could cause degeneration of tooth enamel, if left to build up.

If you live in a city and walk your dog regularly on pavement, chances are that his nails are kept trimmed from the "wear and tear" they receive from the sidewalks. However, if your dog gets all of his exercise in your yard, or if his nails simply grow rather quickly, it will occasionally be necessary for you to clip his nails. It is best for you to have your veterinarian show you the proper way to perform the nail clipping at first. Special care must always be taken to avoid cutting too far and reaching the "quick." If you cut into the quick of the nail, it will bleed, so it is easy to see why an expert must show you the proper procedure. A nail clipper designed especially for dogs can be purchased at any pet shop.

CARE OF THE AGED DOG

With the increased knowledge and care available, there is no reason why your dog should not live to a good old age. As the years go by he may need a little additional care. Remember that an excessively fat dog is not healthy, particularly as he grows older, so limit the older dog's food accordingly. He needs exercise as much as ever, although his heart cannot bear the strain of sudden and violent exertion. Failing eyesight or hearing means lessened awareness of dangers, so you must protect him more than ever.

Should you decide at this time to get a puppy, to avoid being without a dog when your old friend is no longer with you, be very careful how you introduce the puppy. He naturally will be playful and will expect the older dog to respond to his advances. Sometimes the old dog will get a new lease on life from a new puppy, but he may be consumed with jealousy. Do not give the newcomer the attention that formerly was exclusively the older dog's. Feed them apart, and show your old friend that you still love him the most; the puppy, not being accustomed to individual attention, will not mind sharing your love.

TATTOOING

Tattooing is an increasingly popular method of identifying your dog that has met with growing success in assuring the safe return of lost or stolen dogs. Several registries exist that will record a dog's tattoo number along with his owner's name, address and telephone number. Two types of tattoo numbers can be assigned. In the case of mixed breed dogs, the owner's social security number is generally used; in the case of pedigreed dogs, the dog's AKC registration number is used. These two numbers are the most common means of identification. The groin or inside of the ear is the usual spot for the tattoo mark, though cases have been cited in which a dog's ear was cut off to eliminate the possibility of catching the dognappers.

For a minor fee, your veterinarian can do the simple, painless job that may insure the return of a beloved pet or show dog. Such return would be reward enough for the few minutes it takes to have this simple procedure done. Since a puppy grows very rapidly, it is best not to have him tattooed until he is at least four months old to avoid any possible smearing of the tattoo ink. There is almost no danger of infection if the job is done properly and exhibitors run no risk of having the show dog's career impaired by the tattoo mark since the AKC has ruled that no judge may disqualify or penalize a dog because of a tattoo.

Your local kennel club will be able to supply the name of a registry in your area.

9. DOG SHOW COMPETITION

There is no greater pleasure for the owner than showing a beautiful dog perfectly groomed and trained for the show ring. Whether he wins or not, it is gratifying to show a dog in superb condition, one that is a credit to your training and care. A great deal of preparation, both for you and your dog, is needed before the day that you do any serious winning. Showing is not as easy as it looks, even if you have a magnificent dog. He must be presented to the judge so that all of his good points are shown to advantage. This requires practice in gaiting, daily grooming from puppyhood, and the proper diet to make him sound in body.

When you buy your puppy you probably will think he is the best in the country and possibly in the world, but before you enter the highly competitive world of dog shows, get an unbiased expert opinion. Visit a few dog shows as a spectator and make mental notes of what is required of the handlers and dogs. Watch how the experienced handlers manage their dogs to bring out their best points.

HOW TO SELECT A SHOW DOG

If you are planning to show your dog, it is best not to buy a puppy any younger than four or six months of age. Since it is difficult at best to predict what a puppy will look like at maturity, you cannot rely wholly on its appearance while it is only six or eight weeks old. By doing a certain amount of homework before purchasing your show dog, you can be assured to an extent that you will end up with a show quality dog that will hold its own in the show rings. Before going out to buy, read some good books on your breed. Consult a reputable book of standards for the breed to get an idea of what the dog should look like as an adult. Remember that no individual dog ever completely achieves the standard, but knowing the important conformational points of the breed will help to illustrate what you are aiming for in your show dog. Attending dog shows and talking with veterans who have been in the dog game for a while will give you valuable information to use when choosing your own show prospect.

One of the best assurances you can get in a field where there are no real guarantees is to search out well-known breeders who are known to have successfully bred show winners through several generations. Ask to look at the pedigree of any puppy you are considering buying, noting whether there are numerous top-quality dogs in the ancestry. Have the sire and

When you purchase your puppy, the breeder can supply you with a pedigree for him. A puppy of champion bloodlines is often of superior quality.

dam of the litter you are interested in been bred before, and if so, what was the overall quality of their previous offspring? If they have produced consistently good dogs through several of the same pairings, your chances of getting a good specimen are fairly high. If the stud or bitch, or both, are unproven in previous litters, the probability of attaining top quality in the puppies is less likely.

In general, the rule of thumb to follow is to go by the expertise of the breeder. A reputable breeder will sell you the best dog possible if you make it clear to him that the dog will definitely be used for a show career. The show contender you purchase not only represents you as its owner, but also reflects the quality of the kennel of the breeder. The reputation of both exhibitor and breeder is made by the quality of the dogs they present, so careful selection of a show dog is essential to all involved.

TYPES OF DOG SHOWS

There are various types of dog shows. The American Kennel Club sanctioned matches are shows at which purebred dogs may compete, but not for championship points. These are excellent for you to enter to accustom you and your dog to showing. If your dog places in a few match shows, then you might seriously consider entering the big-time shows. An American Kennel Club all-breed show is one at which purebred dogs compete for championship points. An American Kennel Club specialty show is for one breed only. It may be held in conjunction with an all-breed show (by designating the classes at that show as its specialty show) or it may be held entirely apart. Obedience trials are different in that in them the dog is judged according to his obedience and ability to perform, not by his conformation to the breed standard.

There are two types of championship conformation shows: *benched* and *unbenched*. At a benched show your dog must be on his appointed bench during the advertised hours of the show's duration. He may be removed from the bench only to be taken to the exercise pen or to be groomed (an hour before the showing) in an area designated for handlers to set up their crates and grooming tables. At an unbenched show your car may serve as a bench for your dog.

To become a champion your dog must win fifteen points in competition with other dogs; a portion of the fifteen points must be awarded as major point wins (three to five points) under different judges.

This scene from a large indoor show captures the exciting moment when the group winners go before the judge for the Best In Show competition.

HOW TO ENTER

If your dog is purebred and registered with the AKC—or eligible for registration—you may enter him in the appropriate show class for which his age, sex, and previous show record qualify him. You will find coming shows listed in the different dog magazines or at your petshop. Write to the secretary of the show, asking for the premium list. When you receive the entry form, fill it in carefully and send it back with the required entry fee. Then, before the show, you should receive your exhibitor's pass, which will admit you and your dog to the show. Here are the five official show classes:

PUPPY CLASS: Open to dogs at least six months and not more than twelve months of age. Limited to dogs whelped in the United States and Canada.

NOVICE CLASS: Open to dogs six months of age or older that have never won a first prize in any class other than puppy class, and less than three first prizes in the novice class itself. Limited to dogs whelped in the United States or Canada.

BRED BY EXHIBITOR CLASS: Open to all dogs, except cham-

To transport your dog long distances, crates should be used that have been made especially for that purpose. They are designed to give your dog optimum ventilation and comfort, while still assuring his maximum safety and protection.

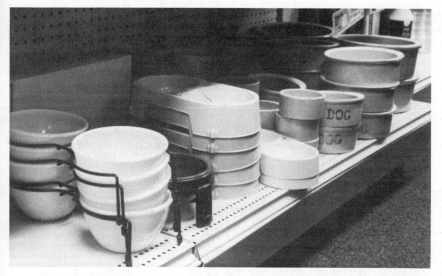

Your pet store carries a large number of pet feeding and watering bowls, in sizes suitable for any size dog. While at a show, be sure to supply your dog with a light meal and some fresh water to keep him comfortable.

pions, six months of age or over which are exhibited by the same person, or his immediate family, or kennel that was the recognized breeder on the records of the American Kennel Club.

AMERICAN-BRED CLASS: Open to dogs that are not champions, six months of age or over, whelped in the United states after a mating which took place in the United States.

OPEN CLASS: Open to dogs six months of age or over, with no exceptions.

In addition there are local classes, the Specials Only class, and brace and team entries.

For full information on dog shows, read the book *How to Show Your Own Dog,* by Virginia Tuck Nichols. (T.F.H.)

JUNIOR SHOWMANSHIP

If you have considered that you and your dog are going to go the show route, you might consider having your youngster show the dog in the ring. If your child has an especially good relationship with his pet, or if he has trained the dog himself, as many children do, then Junior Showmanship might be a good learning experience.

Junior Showmanship is competition among children of different age groups, handling dogs owned by their immediate families. The age divisions are: Novice A, for 10 to 12 year olds; Novice B, for those boys and girls from 13 to 16 (entrants in these two classes must have one or no prior Junior Showmanship wins); Open A for those 10 to 12 years of age; Open B for those 13 to 16 (these entrants must have earned two or more Junior Showmanship awards).

Children involved in JS have the wonderful opportunity to feel a sense of achievement and victory, should they walk away with the ribbons after a show. Even still, winning is not the most important factor here: the pride and responsibility the youngster feels at having reached the ring is surely worth the effort and discipline required to enter showmanship competition.

For more information on JS, and to obtain a rules and regulations booklet, you can contact the American Kennel Club in New York.

ADVANCED PREPARATION

Before you go to a show your dog should be trained to gait at a trot beside you, with head up and in a straight line. In the ring you will have to gait your dog around the edge with other dogs and then individually up and down the center runner. In addition the dog must stand for ex-

If yours is intended to be a show dog, you will want to be prepared with all the tools and equipment necessary for the meticulous grooming of a show dog. Several different types of combs, brushes, clippers and coat grooming products can be obtained from the local pet store.

Be sure to take along a comfortable carrier for your dog if he is to be confined, or benched, during the show's duration.

amination by the judge, who will look at him closely and feel his head and body structure. He should be taught to stand squarely, hind feet slightly back, head up on the alert. Showing requires practice training sessions in advance. Get a friend to act as judge and set the dog up and "show" him a few minutes every day.

Sometime before the show, give your dog a bath so he will look his best. Get together all the things you will need to take to the show. You will want to take a water dish and a bottle of water for your dog (so he won't be affected by a change in drinking water). Take your show lead, bench chain (if it is a benched show), combs and brush, and the identification ticket sent by the show superintendent, noting the time you must be there and the place where the show will be held, as well as the time of judging.

THE DAY OF THE SHOW

Don't feed your dog the morning of the show, or give him at most a light meal. He will be more comfortable in the car on the way, and will show more enthusiastically. When you arrive at the show grounds, find out where he is to be benched and settle him there. Your bench or stall

Conformation to the ideal standard for the breed will be recognized in show dogs by the awarding of ribbons and trophies. Dog show entrants can win on several different levels, with the most significant and exciting award being Best In Show honors.

number is on your identification ticket, and the breed name will be on placards fastened to the ends of the row of benches. Once you have your dog securely fastened to his stall by a bench chain (use a bench crate instead of a chain if you prefer), locate the ring where your dog will be judged (the number and time of showing will be on the program of judging which came with your ticket). After this you may want to take your dog to the exercise ring to relieve himself, and give him a small drink of water. Your dog will have been groomed before the show, but give him a final brushing just before going into the show ring. When your breed judging is called, it is your responsibility to be at the ringside ready to go in. The steward will give you an armband which has on it the number of your dog.

Then, as you step into the ring, try to keep your knees from knocking! Concentrate on your dog and before you realize it you'll be out again, perhaps back with the winners of each class for more judging and finally, with luck, it will be over and you'll have a ribbon and trophy—and, of course, the most wonderful dog in the world!

10. BUILDING A KENNEL AND EXERCISE RUNS

DRAWING UP PLANS

Whether you have one dog or many, the time may come when you decide that an outdoor kennel and runs will best satisfy your dog's exercise and housing needs. Properly built and maintained, a kennel offers your dog the comfort of dry living quarters, adequate ventilation and sunlight, and the availability of regular exercise.

Before you begin to draw up plans for kennel construction, check with your town's municipal offices to see if a building permit is required and which, if any, regulations of the building code you must adhere to. The permit, if required, must be obtained before any construction is begun. Building a kennel is not a small undertaking, so pre-planning on all fronts will prevent unexpected snags from cropping up, causing time delays and inconveniences.

One of the first decisions to make concerns the choice between building the kennel yourself as a sort of family project, or hiring a general contractor to do the work. If you decide on the latter, details of financing, building plans and blueprints to suit your needs should be worked out before contractual agreements are signed. For the plans on actual construction, including a concrete foundation, framework and overall structure, you should consult an architect who will, for a fee, draw up a set of blueprints for you or a contractor to follow. Have the architect see your land, and detail clearly to him each specific feature you want designed into the building. In this way you will enable him to set down a precise set of blueprints, meeting your specifications.

LAND AND SPACE REQUIREMENTS

To build an average size kennel, you must have a significant parcel of land to set aside for this purpose. The location of the building site should provide adequate sunlight and shade for warmth and coolness throughout the seasons. The soil should be of a high gravel content as a gravel soil provides good drainage. By comparison, a sandy soil, though its surface dries quickly, retains dampness and residual dirt just beneath the surface. It is also a favorite breeding place of fleas and similar pests.

Drainage is a prime consideration, not only to let natural ground water run off, but also to let the water drain off from the frequent hosings a kennel must be given to ensure cleanliness and prevent growth of disease-producing germs. A kennel should be trenched for drainage much the way a soldier trenches around his tent. One continuous drainage ditch approximately eight inches wide should be dug around all sides of the kennel, no further than a foot away from the kennel walls. It should be dug to a depth of four inches to start with, sloping an additional inch for every three yards of land. With ditches extending from at least two front corners of the building down to this surrounding ditch, water will run away from the building to the lowest point of land, preventing moisture build-up or preventing the water to lay near the kennel building itself. The drainage system can be sophisticated further, the ditch tiled, for instance, and eventually connecting with or running to a storm drain. Whatever else is devised, drainage should definitely figure into your building plans.

BUILDING MATERIALS

The building materials you use are of great importance. Not only must they be of good quality but they must be of a type that will protect the dog from the elements. For example, sheet metal, a conductor of both heat and cold, should never be used for the outside walls or ceilings. It becomes extremely hot in the sun and will retain heat in the kennel, making a potentially dangerous and certainly uncomfortable situation for the dogs. Outside walls should ideally be constructed from lumber, bricks or cinder blocks. The walls must be insulated with a substance that will serve equally well in all seasons, protecting your dogs from the heat and the cold.

Interior walls can be constructed of wood, plywood or plaster board. Plywood has the advantage of being extremely durable; however, plywood is quite expensive and can give way to splintering should the dogs scratch at it. Plaster board, also commonly known as sheet rock, is inexpensive and relatively durable. Plaster board does not, however, stand up well to moisture, but more than compensates for this drawback by being very resistant to insect and rodent infestation.

The above plans detail the probable steps involved in the construction of a rather large kennel, suited for up to a dozen dogs. At first, most dog owners have only one or two dogs that they want to provide for. If this is the case, a large dog house, modified somewhat, will aptly serve until such time that a larger kennel is needed.

THE SINGLE DOG HOUSE

While a dog will be contented with less living space than his master is accustomed to, his own house should be large enough to allow for free space around and above him when he stands up in the enclosure. The size of the dog house depends, of course, on the size of the dog.

Using materials purchased from any lumber store, you can build a dog house yourself. When constructing the house, take care to finish it off well, leaving no nails or wood splinters protruding from the wood which could injure the dog.

If you wish to move your pet into a new, ready-to-go home, finished dog houses can be purchased in varying styles and price ranges. Your pet shop may have some houses in stock; if not, the owner can probably suggest an outlet where one would be available. The yellow pages of your phone directory may also be useful in locating an establishment that carries dog houses, either constructed or in kits. Some of the latest styles available are quite pleasing to the eye, such as the house constructed out of unstripped logs, designed to give your dog his own little log cabin! If you check various outlets you will find that dog houses range in design from the simple to the elaborate.

CARE OF THE DOG HOUSE

To prevent dampness and to retain heat in the dog house, it should not be placed directly on the ground, but elevated at least several inches. A 2" x 4" beam placed under two opposing sides of the house, with the 4" side lying flat on the ground, should allow for proper ventilation beneath the structure. However, in winter months you will want to close off this space to prevent drafts. In this case, boards can easily and quickly be nailed between the 2" x 4"'s already in place to cover the exposed openings. Keeping the dog house a proper distance from the ground also serves to prevent the possibility of water damage, which will cause the wood to warp and eventually decay. Infestation of the wood by insects can be prevented by keeping the primary wood of the house from contact with the dirt below.

Whether kept in the yard or in the garage, the single dog house has the advantage of being able to be moved from spot to spot. Moving the dog house will be necessary occasionally for such reasons as cleaning, moving into or out of direct sunlight or shade, etc. This is an advantage when you consider that in the cold winter months your dog may very much appreciate having his house placed in direct sunlight! In cold weather the dog house can be positioned with the entranceway facing east or south, to receive full sunlight.

If a shifting of position is all that is needed, a strong friend or two should be able to help relocate the house. However, if the move is for a considerable distance and your dog house is quite heavy, a moving dolly may be necessary.

113

←1

2

(1) A wire crate is needed for dog shows and for traveling. (2) An action photo shows an Ibizan jumping and fetching. (3) Snoozing for awhile is the young Gyrfalcon, owned by Charlotte Schwartz.

3

11. AKC RECOGNITION FOR THE IBIZAN

Needless to say, now that the Ibizan Hound has become a member of the Hound Group at the dog shows, we will be seeing more and more of them in the show rings. Many dedicated breeders and exhibitors have cause to celebrate this fact, as due to the unrelenting efforts of the early pioneers in the breed recognition became a reality in January, 1979.

The breed owes its acceptance to the Seoanes, the Preus, Stetson Kennedy, Ron and Judy Bauer, Richard and Laura Edwards, Dixon Smith, Mrs. William Prescott, John Goodwin, Helen Peck, the Lyman Porters, William H. O'Brien and Mrs. Lee F. Tripp. These fanciers started the ball rolling and captured the interest of those who were to join their ranks and carry the breed even further.

In this development of the breed, the name of Peg Hamilton Ozlek comes to mind. A club officer and columnist for the breed in *Popular Dogs* magazine, she is still active with the club newsletter. Susan Stafford and Nan Kilgore Koppel have contributed their artistic talents to the newsletter, as well as having bred and shown some exquisite Ibizans. Georgianna Mueller, Pamela Woicicki, D.M. Kochajda, W.R. Reynolds, Mrs. W.C. Thompson and Clarence F. Gaines, originator of Gaines Dog Food are a few others whose names are associated with the establishment of the breed.

Roland D. Sourdy and Allan Reznik were active in the breed in Canada. By 1979, Ibizan Hounds were being spotted at shows all over the United States, Puerto Rico, the Virgin Islands, and in Mexico. In England they were shown in the Variety Classes at Crufts and more extensively at the shows sponsored by the British Hound Association.

Long before July 1, 1968 when the Ibizans were permitted to compete in the Miscellaneous Classes at the American Kennel Club shows, advocates of the breed were paving the way for complete recognition by winning honors at the American Sighthound Field Association events. A big step toward the ultimate goal of complete acceptance in all phases of the dog game was reached when Dean Wright's "Eterna of Treybeau" became the first Ibizan Hound to gain the title of Field Champion.

Dean Wright continues to be active in the breed and has served as president of the Ibizan Hound Club of the United States, as it is now known. The club newsletter is called *The Third Eye*.

The Ibizan Hound Club of the United States is particularly anxious to educate the public about this comparatively "rare" breed that has entered

The first litter of Ibizan puppies registered with the American Kennel Club after recognition. Janis Copenhaver is pictured with Sunking Eterna of Treybeu's sleepy, yawning triplets!

the arena. The club will be sponsoring match shows, and specialty shows are planned.

Membership in a club devoted exclusively to a single breed is an essential part of owning a dog. All available information is furnished through the activities of the club, and it is an excellent way to unite owners, breeders and exhibitors to insure a safe future for the dogs. Parent clubs are a guard against indiscriminate and unknowledgeable breeders who might want to "jump on the bandwagon" with the increasing popularity of this fascinating "new" breed.

The years ahead will undoubtedly present all sorts of exciting challenges and triumphs for the Ibizan Hounds, and we can look forward to great success for this wonderful breed, which boasts one of the richest and oldest heritages in the world of dogs.

▲1

▼2

3

(1) A hound glove is useful in removing stray hairs and fostering a sheen in the coat. (2) Here, a hound glove used on a leg. (3) Take care to gently wipe any secretions that form in the corners of your dog's eyes. (4) A nail clipper like the one in chapter eight is useful in keeping the nails trimmed.

4

12. THE PHARAOH HOUND: SIMILARITIES TO THE IBIZAN

It is easy to see—and to understand—why there is so much confusion in determining which of the slender, big-eared dogs are Ibizan Hounds and which are Pharaoh Hounds when the two breeds mingle at dog shows, in the fields, or on lure coursing tracks. When a dog fancier actually tries to determine "which is which," the differences become a little more obvious, however.

Ibizans, officially recognized by the AKC in January, 1979, are usually white with patterns of red, while the Pharaoh Hounds are solid red in color. There is also a difference in size, with the Pharaoh Hound, a member of the Miscellaneous Class, being those of smaller stature.

The similarities of the breeds are much more numerous and clearly evident. Both of these magnificent breeds have a claim to fame with their ancestry dating back to the earliest days in Egypt, and they can boast of having had their images carved on the walls of the ancient pharaohs' tombs. Both are among the oldest breeds of dogs known to man.

Both breeds were eventually transported to various Mediterranean islands by the merchants and traders who carried goods between Egypt and a host of foreign ports. While the Ibizan finally took hold in Ibiza and claimed it as its native land, the Pharaoh Hound can be traced back to the island of Gozo, where it prospered as that island's leading hunting dog.

Pharaoh Hounds are recognized as sight and scent hunters and are noted for their speed and agility. They were first brought to the attention of the dog fancy in England in 1963 and found their way to America by 1967, where they have since made a slow but steady increase in popularity. Their success in obedience training circles, top-winning performances in the field and excellence at lure coursing competitions have earned them a reputation as the ideal all-around canine companion. Their field championship titles won in stiff competition with all the other sight hounds has earned them additional respect and popularity.

Through the endeavors and devotion of the Pharaoh Hound Club of America the breed has been accepted for competition at AKC-approved dog shows in the Miscellaneous Breeds classes as of January 1, 1979. As the Ibizan Hound moved up into the regular championship classes on that date, the Pharaoh Hounds could be said to have "moved into their

The resemblance of the Pharaoh Hound to the Ibizan is clearly seen in this picture of Briling Zahara. This magnificent red bitch was a show winner on her native Mediterranean island of Gozo, where the Pharaoh Hound originated.

position" as one of the most active breeds in the Miscellaneous Class and will not be competing for long in the Miscellaneous Class. It is believed to be a good omen for their receiving full AKC recognition in the near future.

The devoted advocates of the Pharaoh Hound are prone to refer to their favorite breed as "The Pharaoh Hound: an ancient breed whose time has come . . ."

THE PHARAOH HOUND STANDARD

With slight variations on the English Standard for the Pharaohs, the Pharaoh Hound Club of America composed a standard for the breed, which we present here to best illustrate the differences between the Ibizan and the Pharaoh. We believe that the standard will prove interesting to those interested in either or both breeds.

In judging the Pharaoh Hounds at match shows or in the Miscellaneous Classes judges must hold this Standard to be a description of the *ideal* Pharaoh Hound, and any deviation from it calls for the dogs being judged to be penalized to the extent of the deviation.

(1) Some simple obedience commands are easily learned if taught with patience and persistence. In this photo, Charlotte Schwartz teaches her Gyrfalcon the "sit/stay" hand signal and verbal command. (2) The well-trained Ibizan is one who has learned to "heel" while on lead (leash). (3) Striking a majestic pose: Gyrfalcon at rest in a field during an exercise outing.

▲2

▼3

The beautiful "Eterna," the Ibizan Hound breed's first field champion and the first AKC breed champion. Co-owned by Kathy O'Brien and Dean Wright. Note the similarities between this Ibizan and the written standard for the Pharaoh Hound.

STANDARD FOR THE PHARAOH HOUND

BREED STANDARD—The Pharaoh Hound is of great antiquity, being one of the earliest breeds in recorded history. The breed is virtually unchanged today from the painting, reliefs and sculptures found in the tomb chapels and temples of the Ancient Egyptians—some as much as 5,000 years old.

The Pharaoh Hound is medium sized, of noble bearing with hard clean cut lines—graceful, well balanced, very fast with free easy movement and alert expression.

CHARACTER—Intelligent, friendly, affectionate and playful. Alert and active. Very fast with a marked keenness for hunting, both by sight and scent.

The general appearance is one of grace, power and speed.

HEAD AND SKULL—Skull long, lean and chiseled. Foreface slightly longer than the skull. Only slight stop. Top of the skull parallel with the foreface representing a blunt wedge.

MOUTH—Powerful jaws with strong teeth. Scissor bite.

NOSE—Flesh coloured, blending with the coat. No other colour.

EYES—Amber coloured blending with coat, oval moderately deep set with keen intelligent expression.

EARS—Medium high set, carried erect when alert, but very mobile, broad at the base, fine and large.

NECK—Long, lean and muscular with a slight arch to carry the head on high. Clean throat line.

FOREQUARTERS—Shoulders long and sloping and well-laid back. Strong without being loaded. Forelegs straight and parallel. Elbows well tucked in. Pasterns strong. Body lithe with almost straight top-line. Slight slope from croup to root of tail. Deep brisket almost down to point of elbow. Ribs well sprung. Moderate tuck up. Length of body from breast to haunch bone slightly longer than height of withers to ground.

HINDQUARTERS—Strong and muscular. Moderate sweep of stifle. Well developed second thigh. Limbs parallel.

FEET—Neither cat nor hare but strong, well knuckled and firm, turning neither in nor out. Paws well padded. Dew claws may be removed.

TAIL—Medium set—fairly thick at the base and tapering whip-like, reaching below the point of hock in repose. Well carried and curved when in action. The tail should not be tucked between the legs. A screw tail is a fault.

GAIT—Free and flowing; the head should be held fairly high and the dog should cover the ground well without any apparent effort. The legs and feet should move in line with the body; any tendency to throw the feet sideways, or a high stepping "hackney" action is a definite fault.

COAT—Short and glossy, ranging from fine and close to slightly harsh with no feathering.

COLOUR—Ranging from tan/rich tan/chestnut with white markings allowed as follows:

White tip on tail strongly desired.

White on chest (called "the Star")

White on toes and slim white snip on center line of face permissible.

Flecking or other white undesirable.

RECOMMENDED HEIGHT—DOGS—58 cm—63 cm (23 inches—25 inches).

BITCHES—53 cm—61 cm (21 inches—24 inches) ALL-OVER BALANCE MUST BE MAINTAINED.

Accident blemishes should not be considered as faults.

The foregoing description is that of the ideal Pharaoh Hound. Any deviation from the above-described dog must be penalized to the extent of the deviation.

As accepted by: The Pharaoh Hound Club of America.